WITNESS TO HISTORY

WITNESS TO HISTORY

Transition and Transformation of India, 1947–1964

OXFORD
UNIVERSITY PRESS

Oxford University Press is a department of the University of Oxford.
It furthers the University's objective of excellence in research, scholarship,
and education by publishing worldwide. Oxford is a registered trademark of
Oxford University Press in the UK and in certain other countries

Published in India
by Oxford University Press
YMCA Library Building, 1, Jai Singh Road, New Delhi 110 001, India

© Oxford University Press 2011

ISBN-13: 978-0-19-807434-2
ISBN-10: 0-19-807434-4

Typeset in Berling LT STD 10/14.8
by Sai Graphic Design, New Delhi 110 055
Printed in India at Artxel, New Delhi 110 020

Contents

Acknowledgements

This publication is the brainchild of Shri R.D. Pradhan, Vice Chairman, Nehru Centre. He conceptualized the theme, selected the resource persons and used his good offices to invite some of them to the Centre to deliver a lecture. Those who could not come were kind enough to send us their written pieces. I am deeply indebted to Shri Pradhan for his efforts and also to the distinguished contributors.

My special thanks to Ms Sonia Khare for copyediting the text. Our librarian, Mrs Arati Desai and the entire team of Nehru Centre deserve congratulations for the publication of this volume.

I.M. KADRI
General Secretary
Nehru Centre

Acknowledgements

This publication is the result of Shaukat Dewan...

Introduction

The Nehru era (1947–1964) will always be considered crucial in the history of independent India. It was a period when transfer of power took place from the British to Indian hands; the country was partitioned and millions of refugees had to be rehabilitated. Gandhi was assassinated within six months of independence. Sardar Patel ably integrated 565 princely states into the Indian union. The interim government was formed in September 1946 and from then onwards till 27 May 1964, Jawaharlal Nehru, the first Prime Minister of independent India, was the sole arbiter of India's national programme.

The first five years of independence were most difficult for India and Nehru's greatest contribution in those trying years was to keep together this large and diverse country. The framing of the Constitution of India also happened during the first five years and so did Pakistan's foiled attempt to seize Srinagar by force.

Democracy took root in India. The people of India were empowered at one stroke, which was an unprecedented happening. Three peaceful general elections were held on the basis of adult suffrage. Nehru nurtured democracy and established healthy parliamentary practices. He was particular about his attendance in the parliament and never missed the question hour. He accorded utmost courtesy to the Speaker of the Lok Sabha, the opposition, and the treasury benches, and gracefully accepted any logical point of view emanating from the opposition. Nehru supported Private Members' Bills that has now become a rarity in the Parliament. Secularism was an article of faith with him and even his worst detractors acknowledged that.

The basic foundation of industry, science, and technology was laid by Nehru; he introduced planning and advocated mixed economy; his role in laying the foundation of the three national academies—Sahitya Akademi, Lalit Kala Akademi, and Sangeet Natak Akademi—for the promotion of art and literature was pivotal.

Nehru had his own vision of international order. Capitalism had no place in that order as it was the cause of exploitation and oppression. He visualized an international order based on truth, justice, and fairplay. He enunciated the doctrine of Panchsheel, the five principles of peaceful coexistence, and vigorously campaigned for disarmament and against regional military pacts. His policy of non-alignment was a strategy to prevent the spread of the Cold War to those Afro-Asian nations which had gained their freedom from colonial rule.

But conceding suzerainty to China over Tibet without first settling the border problem with the former was a grave error of judgement. It was Nehru's failure in gauging China's assertive stance on its territorial claims that eventually led to a conflict resulting in India's humiliation. It also caused tremendous damage to Nehru's prestige and stature internationally.

Nehru is held responsible for the intractable Kashmir problem which has been a drain on the country's resources. In people's perception it was a mistake to agree to a 'cease-fire' without first driving out the raiders from all parts of Kashmir; it was also a mistake to refer the matter to the United Nations (UN) under Chapter VI of the Charter and make Kashmir a disputed territory, particularly after it had acceded to India; and worst of all to suggest 'plebiscite under the UN auspices'. These three alleged mistakes have been debated at length in the pages that follow.

It is fashionable these days to denigrate Nehru. The fact, however, is that he, with all his possible drawbacks, made an amazingly versatile contribution to the making of modern India.

Fortunately, we have in our midst, persons who have been witness to the making of history in the Nehruvian era and who, in their own way, made a contribution in shaping its course. Their reminiscences, recollections, and interpretations of events based on personal knowledge and their interactions with Nehru should be most valuable to historiography. These witnesses to that era could make a unique contribution to the history of that period. Nehru Centre has attempted to preserve this wealth of knowledge for posterity through a series of articles and lectures titled 'Witness to History: Transition and Transformation of India (1947–1964)' which have been compiled in this book.

P.C. Alexander is one of the most distinguished and respected public servants of the post-independence era. As an outstanding statesman, he has the distinction of having held several high positions in public life, both at the national and international level. He looks at Nehru's contributions as a leader in the freedom struggle and as a nation-builder, and in spite of being an ardent admirer of Nehru he hopes to be as objective as possible in his comments and observations. He deals with some of the most salient features of the Nehru era which he has divided into three phases—1946–50, 1951–60, and 1961–4. While talking about these phases, he also talks at length about Nehru's socialism, his foreign policy, and the steps he took for the modernization of India. He concludes by saying that Nehru was a rare combination of a good administrator and a good human being.

Karan Singh is a senior member of the Indian National Congress. He has been actively engaged in politics and had the privilege of a very close association with Pandit Jawaharlal Nehru. In fact, he looked upon Nehru as his political guru. In his article, Singh mentions some main events of that era in which Jawaharlal Nehru played a major role. These include the Partition, the framing of the Constitution, the integration of the Indian states, the formation of linguistic states, planning, community development, science and technology, and foreign affairs. After giving his views on Nehru's role in each of these issues, Karan Singh concludes that Nehru can rightly be called the Father of the Indian State.

Subhash Kashyap is a former Secretary General of the Lok Sabha, a well-known political scientist, and an expert in constitutional law. At the very outset, Kashyap clarifies that his recollections of Nehru are only those of a child who was privileged to see him from near, of a student activist who had a few occasions to meet and talk to him, and lastly of a young parliamentary officer in Delhi who saw him function in the Parliament during 1953–64. Kashyap's narration of his interactions with Nehru tells us more about Nehru the human being and how he inspired the young and the old around him. Kashyap has an interesting anecdotal style which makes for easy reading.

Muchkund Dubey confesses that his acquaintance with Pandit Jawaharlal Nehru was almost non-existent and his contacts with him were of an impersonal and fleeting nature. But from whatever he saw, he was convinced that very few of Nehru's contemporaries were as acutely conscious of the changes taking place around them and as constantly engaged in sifting and evaluating them with a view to formulating and adjusting policies, as was Panditji. He goes on to describe in detail Nehru's vision of the international order. At the end of his writing he says that the world situation today is much less conducive to the realization of the international order of Nehru's vision than it was during his time. He poses the question, 'Should we then dismiss Nehru's vision of the international order as utopian and unrealizable?' And answers in the same breath, 'Nehru himself would not have reconciled to the *status quo* ... he would have continued to strive for the realization of his vision of the world order with greater courage of conviction, firmer determination, and renewed vigour.'

Jagmohan has held the post of the Governor of Jammu and Kashmir twice and has been instrumental in providing capable administration to the state. In his article, he focuses mainly on 'Nehru and Cities' and 'Nehru and Kashmir' and in this context speaks about Nehru's impact on his own work first as a city planner and administrator and then as Governor of Jammu and Kashmir. In the section on cities he talks about Nehru's influence on the Delhi Master Plan, his love for Shahjahanabad, for architecture, and his views on slum eradication. In the section on Kashmir, Jagmohan talks about the internal and external aspects of the Kashmir issue, and finally about Nehru's deep and abiding relationship with Kashmir.

Balraj Puri is one of the most widely published political commentators in the country. He mediated the famous Sheikh Abdullah-Indira Gandhi accord. From India's first Prime Minister Jawaharlal Nehru to the present Prime Minister Manmohan Singh, Puri has been constantly consulted on various aspects of the Kashmir issue. In his article, Puri deals elaborately with Nehru's Kashmir policy. He talks about what the people of Jammu wanted as well as Nehru's relationship with Sheikh Abdullah, among other things. He ends his article with the thought that had Nehru lived a little longer, he would have settled the Kashmir problem almost permanently.

Inder Malhotra is one of the most respected journalists of India. He has been a syndicated columnist since taking premature retirement from his post of Editor of *The Times of India*, New Delhi (1978–86). As mentioned earlier, it has become fashionable these days to denigrate Nehru. Malhotra, in pursuit of the theme, tries to explain the paradox of the contribution of Nehru in the formation and development of free India into a nation state, and that of 'Nehru-bashing', as he calls it. He presents his explanation to those who criticize Nehru's policies. He ends by quoting three important personalities and their views on Nehru.

K. Natwar Singh is a senior Indian politician and foreign affairs expert. It is thus befitting that his article should be titled 'A Brief Survey of Jawaharlal Nehru's Foreign Policy'. He states at the beginning that his short essay is not a comprehensive or scholarly assessment of Jawaharlal Nehru's foreign policy. Rather it is a brief, tentative survey in which he has reflected on a few of his more substantial policy concerns and preoccupations. Singh dwells in detail on Nehru's policy of non-alignment, his policies towards USA, USSR, and China. This is, indeed, a succinct analysis of Nehru's foreign policy. However, Singh ends his piece with the concluding remarks—'He was a remarkable Prime Minister. He was a statesman of high standing. He was a humanist. Was he a great Foreign Minister? The jury is still out.'

M.V. Kamath, the senior Indian journalist and former Chairman of Prasar Bharati, in his article, talks about the few interactions he had with Nehru as a young journalist. Kamath and his friends' adventurous meeting with Nehru in a train makes for very interesting reading. In a very lucid manner, he recalls his experiences as the UN correspondent of the Press Trust of India and later when he covered the first Non-Aligned Conference in Belgrade in 1961. Kamath wonders about Nehru's reluctance to meet Indian journalists serving abroad for Indian newspapers. He lists a few mistakes which, according to him, Nehru committed. He, however, ends by stating that to have come of age around 1935 and been a witness to the political scene in India right up to Nehru's death, has been a rich experience.

It is hoped that this endeavour to record the experiences of these personalities will be appreciated and that it will present to the readers, young and old, a rare opportunity to know more about the towering personality of Pandit Jawaharlal Nehru.

P.C. ALEXANDER

1

Jawaharlal Nehru

The Leader and Nation-Builder

For a good part of the Nehru administration, I was a civil servant in Delhi and had the opportunity of observing at close quarters and also participating to some extent in the momentary events of that period. Ever since my student days I have been an ardent admirer of Jawaharlal Nehru. My admiration for this great personality had gone up several-fold when I read his autobiography. The story of his enormous sacrifice for the cause of the country's freedom, his impeccable integrity and nobility of character, his deep erudition and intellectual achievements, and the versatility of his talents and interests had created an indelible impression on my young mind.

For most people of my generation, Jawaharlal was a hero with a capital 'H', but the younger generation which had only read about him could be more detached in its appraisal of the Nehru era. Even people of my generation have at this distance of time and with the benefit of a lot of hindsight developed a more objective and even a critical attitude about his role in Indian administration. I will also try to be as objective as possible in my comments and observations about Nehru's contributions as a leader in the struggle for freedom and as a nation-builder.

The subject being too vast, I will deal with some of the most salient features of the period 1946–1964 in this talk. For the convenience of analysts, I shall divide this period into three phases 1946–50, 1951–60 and 1961–4.

The Nehru Era, Phase I: 1946–50

In June 1945, when Jawaharlal Nehru and the senior Indian National Congress leaders came out of their incarceration in the different jails of India, they found the political situation in the country quite different from what it was three years earlier when they were put behind bars. The serious repression unleashed on the people by Viceroy Wavell's administration after the launching of the Quit India Movement had created great resentment among the people against the British government as never before. The Congress leaders found that there was a marked change in the mood of the Muslims, and particularly in their attitude to the Congress. Jinnah fully utilized the absence of the Congress leaders from the scene to spread the poison of communal hatred between Muslims and Hindus. He succeeded to a large extent in convincing the Muslims that their only hope for living with dignity was in establishing a homeland of their own and had put forward the spurious theory in justification of his stand that the Muslims in India constituted a separate nation different from that of the rest of the population. To Nehru the very idea of Muslims being members of another nation was totally contrary to his convictions. He believed that the Muslims were as nationalist in their outlook as the Hindus or members of any other community in India and he could never think that Jinnah's two-nation theory would ever be acceptable to the Muslims. However, he soon realized that his assessment of Jinnah's hold on the Muslim masses was quite wrong and within a very short period after his release from the jail he realized how much the attitude of the Muslims had changed.

During 1945, there were rumblings of discontent among the armed forces and the troops had mutinied at several stations in India refusing to obey orders as their grievances on the rates of demobilization pay, etc., had not been looked into by the authorities. The most serious among the incidents of discontent in the armed forces was the naval mutiny on 19

February 1946 when about 3000 ratings of the Royal Indian Navy hoisted the national flag on their ships and marched through the streets of Bombay (now Mumbai). There was exchange of fire between British troops and the mutineers. Finally, Congress leaders like Sardar Patel and Jawaharlal Nehru succeeded in persuading the ratings to call off the mutiny. The naval mutiny had convinced the British government that the end of the Raj was near and wisdom lay in negotiating an agreed settlement with the Indians for the end of imperial rule in India.

The Conservative government of Winston Churchill had been replaced in London by a Labour government under the leadership of Clement Attlee who along with many of his Cabinet colleagues had been very supportive of the struggle for freedom in India. The new government announced the appointment of a Mission consisting of three Cabinet ministers, Pethick-Lawrence, Stafford Cripps, and A.V. Alexander, with the mandate to hold discussions with the leaders of the political parties in India in order to arrive at a peaceful transfer of power.

The Cabinet Mission arrived in India in April 1946 and quickly plunged into discussions with the leaders of the main political parties, the Congress and the Muslim League. The discussions revealed very soon that the gulf between these two parties had become quite unbridgeable. The British announced a constitutional framework for transfer of power on 16 May 1946, which involved considerable concessions to the Muslim League's demand for a separate state for the Muslims and also accommodation of some of the major demands of the Congress party. According to these proposals the Indian Union would deal with foreign policy, defence, and communications and would have the powers necessary to raise the finances for these subjects. All other powers would vest in the provinces which would be free to form groups and each group could determine the provincial subjects to be taken in common. Pending framing of the Constitution, administration of the country was to be carried on by an interim government having the support of the major political parties.

Both the Congress and the Muslim League accepted the constitutional arrangements proposed by the Cabinet Mission but differences arose between them about the number of members representing Muslims and Hindus in the interim government. Jinnah insisted on parity between caste Hindus and Muslims in the Cabinet. A more serious difference of opinion arose between the League and the Congress on the grouping of the provinces. According to the Cabinet ministers' proposal, Punjab, Sind, and North West Frontier Province would constitute one group, Bengal and Assam another, and the rest of the provinces, the third. Nehru upset the whole scheme by announcing at a press conference that the Constituent Assembly would be a sovereign body and that the Congress was 'not bound by a single thing except that it has decided to go into the Constituent Assembly'. Elaborating this stand further, Nehru later said that the grouping of provinces into three sections may not be a final arrangement and that if provinces like North West Frontier Province or Assam decided not to join the group designated for them, the scheme of groups of provinces would fail. Jinnah took serious offence at this statement and promptly withdrew the League's acceptance of the Cabinet Mission plan. Even senior Congress leaders like Maulana Azad and Sardar Patel were sharply critical of Nehru's stand on this as they felt that it was a new interpretation of the grouping and it provided an opportunity to Jinnah to withdraw his earlier acceptance of the Cabinet Mission plan.

Whatever may be the merit or otherwise of such criticism by Jawaharlal's close friends in the Congress, the fact remains that it created the impression that the Congress was unilaterally withdrawing from a commitment it had made about abiding by the Cabinet Mission plan. A question which continues to be discussed even now is whether Jawaharlal, by his statement on grouping of provinces had destroyed the last chance of preventing the partition of India and preserving its unity. Was he so carried away by his idealism and strong belief in the unity of India that he could not make a realistic assessment of the emerging political situation? If that was so, how could he become convinced about the advisability of accepting partition within so short a time as a few months after making the controversial statement on the grouping of provinces? Those who defend Nehru's stand on grouping maintain that the groups would not in any case have lasted for long and by his opposition to grouping he had actually prevented the balkanization of India into several small states. An impartial judgement on Nehru's action at this juncture has yet to emerge.

After Jinnah announced the withdrawal of the League's acceptance of the Cabinet Mission plan, the political situation started worsening day by day. In mid-August of 1946, the country witnessed one of the most terrible tragedies in the history of modern India namely the Calcutta (now Kolkata) Killings. Jinnah had fixed 16 August 1946 as 'Direct Action Day' and S.H. Suhrawardy, Chief Minister of the Muslim League ministry in Bengal declared it a public holiday in the province. Armed Muslim League groups in Calcutta indulged in loot, arson, and murder on a scale which the city had never seen before resulting in the destruction of properties worth several crores of rupees and the death of thousands of people. The Congress blamed Jinnah for this programme of murder and the British for not sending in armed forces from outside the state to deal with the situation.

The question about the share of the Muslim League and the Congress in the interim government was eventually resolved and a provincial government was sworn in with Jawaharlal as the Vice President of the Executive Council with the portfolio of External Affairs and Commonwealth Relations. The story of the interim government was one of persistent conflicts between the Congress and the League. The communal violence in Bengal was escalating sharply but the state government was unable or unwilling to control it. There were disputes and strong criticisms from the League's ministers on practically every issue on which Nehru and his colleagues wanted to take action. Jinnah was simultaneously engaged in efforts to create divisions within the ranks of the non-League members. On one occasion when both Baldev Singh and he were in London for a conference, Jinnah had a private meeting with Baldev Singh and told him, 'If you persuade the Sikhs to join hands with the Muslim League, we will have a glorious Pakistan, the gates of which will be near about Delhi if not in Delhi itself.' Baldev Singh, of course, did not fall into Jinnah's trap.

By the beginning of January 1947, it became clear that there were no prospects at all of any agreement between the League and the Congress for sharing power in a united India. Jinnah had nominated a few diehard communalists as the League's representatives in the government. They were not even among the top leaders of the League. The only leader from the League with good political credentials in the interim government was Liaquat Ali Khan. But as Finance minister of the Central government he introduced a budget aimed mainly at clipping the wings of the top industrialists and business leaders of India, most of whom were from the non-Muslim communities.

Nehru was so disgusted with the helplessness and frustration in his role as the Vice President in the interim government that he felt that resignation from the government was the only honourable step that he could take. While Nehru and Patel had come to the conclusion that partition of the country on the basis of religion had become inevitable and even necessary to fulfil the aspiration of the people for independence, Gandhiji remained totally irreconciled to the idea of partition. Nehru and Patel believed that by dividing Punjab and Bengal on the basis of communities, they would be reducing the impact of partition, but Gandhiji was not taken fully into confidence on this idea. Gandhiji continued to oppose any decision on the division of the provinces or the country on communal criteria, but was by then a lone crusader for the cause of unity. Nehru and Patel conveyed to the British authorities their willingness to go along with the suggestion of the partition of Punjab and Bengal and of the country as the best in the circumstances prevalent then.

It was on this background that Prime Minister Attlee announced in London that the British would withdraw from India not later than June 1948, after handing over power to the Central government or in some areas to existing provincial governments. Attlee also announced the appointment of Mountbatten as Viceroy and Governor General in the place of Wavell.

There were wild rumours in the Congress that sharp differences had arisen between Nehru and Patel on various important issues and that Jawaharlal might not include Patel in the Cabinet of independent India. But the truth was that on 1 August 1947 he had written to Patel formally inviting him to join the government and he had also taken Patel's advice on the composition of the new Cabinet. Differences if any between them were always on principles and policies and not motivated by power or self-interest. Patel's reply to Nehru's letter of 1 August 1947 is worth quoting here to illustrate this point. Patel wrote: 'My services will be at your disposal, I hope for the rest of my life, and you will have unquestioned loyalty and devotion from me in the cause for which no man in India has sacrificed as much as you have done. Our combination is unbreakable and there lies our strength.'

Jawaharlal not only assigned to Patel the important portfolios of Home, Information and Broadcasting and States but also the designation of Deputy Prime Minister.

The new government swung into action to handle the problem of massive movement of refugees between the two countries after the Partition and the outbreak of communal riots in several places. This serious problem of maintenance of peace within the country, however, did not prevent the government from going ahead with some of the most important tasks facing it on assumption of power. The most important among them were:

1. the completion of the process of framing the Constitution of independent India,
2. the integration of princely states with the sovereign state of India,
3. the creation of the All India Civil Services with the constitutional guarantee for permanency of tenure, and
4. dealing with the problem of incursion of armed tribesmen into Kashmir supported by the Pakistan army in a move to take over the state by force.

The completion of the Constitution-making process by the end of 1949 was one of the greatest achievements of the nation in the post-Independence period. In spite of the turmoil and chaos prevailing in the country following the Partition of Punjab and Bengal and of the country, the framers of the Constitution went ahead with their task with utmost dedication and could present to the nation a Constitution which could ensure India's smooth transition to a free Republic on 26 January 1950.

It is a well-acknowledged fact that in the integration of the princely states and in the creation of the All India Services, Sardar Patel had played a very crucial role. Patel received unstinted support from Nehru in the task of the integration of princely states with the Indian Union. The smoothness and speed with which several hundred princely states were integrated with the Indian Union is an achievement unparalleled in the history of any country and the tributes which have been paid to Sardar Patel for his sagacity, statesmanship, and courage in this matter are, indeed, most well-deserved. With the exception of three states, namely, Kashmir, Hyderabad, and Junagadh, all other states had acceded to the Indian Union by Independence Day. Kashmir, Hyderabad, and Junagadh had to wait for a few days more for their integration.

In the matter of creation of the All India Services, Nehru had some serious reservations to begin with. He had been a trenchant critic of the

ICS in the pre-Independence days and had even called it a 'kept' service. However, it was Patel's strong belief that an All India Civil Service modelled on the ICS was necessary not only for ensuring efficiency and impartiality in administration but also for strengthening the unity and integrity of the country. Nehru realized within a very short period of his being at the head of the administration in independent India, how useful the institution of the All India Services had been in the planning and implementation of various development schemes and above all in protecting the unity and integrity of the nation.

Nehru's action in agreeing to Mountbatten's proposal for referring the issue of accession of Jammu and Kashmir to the Indian nation to the United Nations and in accepting a plebiscite as a solution for the dispute continues to be a subject of controversy even today. Critics of Nehru maintain that the right action for India should have been to deal with the invasion from Pakistan militarily and to eject the intruders by force from the territory of Kashmir. Nehru, however, believed that since justice regarding Pakistani aggression in Kashmir was fully on the side of India, reference to the UN was the right course open to the country. Nehru's expectation that he would be able to deal with the problem with justice and fairness was quite misplaced and he realized that the UN was not that just and fair in its decisions, only after the ceasefire had helped Pakistan to hold on to the territories it had occupied by force in Kashmir.

Most people believe that it was a gross act of folly on the part of Jawaharlal to have agreed to refer the Kashmir issue to the UN or to accept plebiscite as a solution to the dispute on its accession to India. Kashmir continues to be a problem even sixty years after Nehru chose this path.

The Nehru Era, Phase II: 1951–60

The decade 1950 to 1960 can well be described as the golden chapter of the Nehru era. During this period his reputation rose to great heights not only in India but over the entire world. *Harper's Magazine* described him as the most arresting figure on the world political stage since the end of the Churchill-Stalin-Roosevelt era. The *New York Times* acknowledged him as 'one of the world's most important politicians and of the unchallenged rulers of the world, perhaps the only one who ruled by love and not fear. I recall how proud and privileged we, the civil servants working in the government at that time, felt in having as the head of the government a great statesman like Jawaharlal. In sharp contrast to the mood of cynicism among several civil servants today, the civil servants of those years experienced great job satisfaction and were excited at their role as agents of change and progress and enjoyed the full faith of the political leaders under the leadership of one of the greatest statesmen of the world.

In spite of the universal recognition of his greatness as a statesman, Jawaharlal had faced serious difficulties in going ahead with some of his own wishes and inclinations because of opposition from some of his senior colleagues. The most conspicuous case of such limitation was in the choice of the President of the new Republic who was to take office on 26 January 1950. C.R. Rajagopalachari was Nehru's choice as Governor General of India after Mountbatten laid down that office, but when it came to nominating Rajagopalachari as the President of the Republic some of his senior colleagues in the party including Patel threw their support in favour of Rajendra Prasad for the post. Nehru had to agree to the election of Prasad as he realized that it would not be possible to muster enough support for his candidate.

Another important setback for Nehru was when he strongly opposed the proposal to elect Purushottam Das Tandon as the Congress President in 1951. Nehru had considered Tandon as completely out of line with his own thinking about the directions in which the nation should be guided in the next few years. The attempt of Nehru and some like-minded people to get J.B. Kripalani elected as Congress President failed much to the disappointment of Nehru. For a few months he continued as a member of the Working Committee of the Congress with Tandon as President but he resigned along with a few of his friends from the Working Committee stating that it was impossible to work with a person whose political ideology was totally out of tune with his. Patel had passed away in December 1950 and Tandon knew that it would be impossible for him to carry on as President without the support of Nehru. Tandon resigned and Nehru was elected in his place. With this election Nehru got a free hand in the management of both the government and the party.

Jawaharlal's standing in the country was enhanced considerably because of the spectacular victory which the Congress had in the general elections held during 1951–2. As a Returning Officer in these elections first in the then Madras state in 1951 and a few months later in Travancore-Cochin, to which cadre I had been transferred, I had seen how vigorously Nehru had campaigned to get the people's support for the Congress symbol—the cow and the calf. The Congress party was returned to power at the Centre with 364 seats in the Lok Sabha and it was rightly hailed as a personal victory for Jawaharlal.

In spite of his pre-eminent position as the undisputed leader of the Congress and the Government of India, Jawaharlal had shown great deference to the wishes of some of his surviving top colleagues in the party. Maulana Azad was one of them. Nehru was very keen to induct V.K. Krishna Menon into his Cabinet in 1954. But Maulana Azad whom he had consulted, had indicated strong opposition to his proposal because of the allegations of corruption which had been levelled against him in the purchase of jeeps during the period that Menon was High Commissioner for India in London. Azad had told Nehru that he would resign from the Cabinet if Nehru insisted on including Menon. On 12 August 1954, Nehru sent a personal letter in his own handwriting to Maulana Azad pleading with him to withdraw his objection, but the Maulana remained firm. Nehru was too much of a democrat and too much of a gentleman to break his friendship with Azad on this issue. If Nehru had gone ahead with Menon's appointment as Cabinet minister, Azad would have resigned, but most people would have stood behind Nehru on this issue or any issue on which Nehru wanted peoples' support in the mid-1950s.

The second general elections were held in 1956 and as in the elections of 1951, Jawaharlal was the chief campaigner. The impressive victory of the Congress which secured 371 seats in the Lok Sabha added lustre to the reputation of Nehru as the unquestioned leader of the masses in India.

Among the various issues which Jawaharlal had handled during 1950–60, three stand out as the most important and I shall briefly refer to them here. They are (a) acceptance of the policy of the socialistic pattern of development, (b) the shaping of India's foreign policy on the basis of the doctrine of non-alignment, and (c) the modernization of India through comprehensive social and economic reforms.

NEHRU AND SOCIALISM

If one follows the writings and speeches of Nehru ever since his younger days it will become clear that his socialism was different from the classical socialism as understood in Western countries. In Europe socialism was connected to class war but Nehru had said that, 'it was not necessary we should go through the troubles of Europe to achieve our brand of socialist pattern'. It was not the socialism of Marx but the Indian variant of it which was projected by him for building of an egalitarian society where the common man would have adequate opportunities in the production and more importantly, in the sharing of wealth. Ever since his adult days Nehru had been using every opportunity he could get to express his faith in socialism as the means for reducing the inequalities in Indian society and making the goal of Independence more meaningful to the common people. As President of the Lahore session of the Indian National Congress in December 1929, Nehru had explained what exactly he meant by socialism. He said: 'I must frankly confess that I am a socialist and a republican and no believer in kings and princes or in the order which produces the modern kings of industry who have greater power over the lives and fortunes of men than kings of old, and whose methods are as predatory as those of the old feudal aristocracy.' Jawaharlal had faced serious opposition from some of his senior colleagues in the party to the idea of making socialism the guiding policy for development in India. Gandhi himself did not share Nehru's enthusiasm for socialism and had advised him to go cautiously in pushing his ideas on it. Now that he had become the undisputed leader of both the government and the party in the mid-1950s, he did not want to waste any time in implementing the socialist policy which he believed was the best course for India. At the Congress session at Avadi near the then Madras city in January 1955, Jawaharlal succeeded in getting the wholehearted support of the party in favour of his dream of building a socialistic society. Nehru's careful study of the functioning of the communist government in the Soviet Union had convinced him that the socialism of the Marxists was inconsistent with the democratic ideals for which India was seeking its independence. That was why he was a strong opponent of the Communist party in India for whom, according to Nehru, history begins with 1917'.

Jawaharlal believed in planning and considered it as an important tool for achieving the goal of creating a socialistic society. As soon as he joined the interim government he had set up a Planning Advisory Board. The Board had submitted its report in December 1946, but because of Jawaharlal's pre-occupation with transfer of power and its attendant problems the report had not received any attention. At the earliest opportunity after assuming full powers as the Prime Minister of independent India, in 1950, he set up the Planning Commission with himself as Chairman and Gulzarilal Nanda as Deputy Chairman. The Commission submitted a draft outline of the first Five-Year Plan in July 1951, and the final version of the Plan in December 1952. This report reflected Nehru's philosophy on planned development and focused on alleviating the problems of the underprivileged sections of the society.

The Planning Commission has grown in its responsibilities and in its programmes of action and has now become the principal instrument of the government in determining the priorities of development in all sectors. Because of the comprehensive nature of its powers and responsibilities, the working of the Planning Commission has led, to a great extent, to the dilution of the autonomy of the states but people have accepted the role of the Planning Commission, as envisaged by Nehru, without any major changes during the last fifty-eight years after its establishment. It may sound surprising to many that such an organization has been able to wield so much power and authority in planning for the entire country without any constitutional or even statutory backing behind it and its only sanction is a government order. The growth of the Planning Commission should be considered as a great tribute to the wisdom and foresight of its founder, Jawaharlal Nehru.

NEHRU AND FOREIGN POLICY

Right from the days of the interim government till the end of his life in 1964, Nehru had retained with him the portfolio of India's External Relations. With his deep interest in international affairs and thorough grasp of the problems of the different regions and the important countries of the world, he had been the acknowledged expert on foreign policy matters even before becoming the minister in charge of it in the interim government. The first major initiative he had taken in the area of foreign relations was the convening of an Asian Relations Conference in Delhi in September 1946. It was a non-official conference representative of all shades of opinion in the countries of Asia (Egypt was an invitee) and it proved to be a grand success. It lasted for 10 days from 23 March 1946, and by the time it ended, India had acquired the status of a natural centre of resurgent Asia, forging links of co-operation among most Asian countries.

After Independence Nehru became the acknowledged leader of the Non-aligned Movement along with Marshal Tito of Yugoslavia and Gamal Nasser of Egypt. For Nehru the Non-aligned Movement was not a mere medium for cooperation among the countries of the world which had newly become independent, but a powerful moral force in order to prevent the economic subordination of these countries to the two blocs of the advanced world headed by the United States and the Soviet Union respectively. It was Nehru's firm belief that the developing countries which had succeeded in throwing off their colonial yoke stood in real danger of a new variant of colonialism by the two powerful blocs of developed countries and that their strength depended on collective cooperation.

A fierce Cold War between the two blocs was in full swing in the 1950s. The United States had launched a massive campaign to enlist the support of the newly independent countries for the stand of the Western bloc through devices like formation of regional military pacts and liberal economic aid to these countries. The United States had at that time in its Secretary of State, Dulles, an uncompromising Cold War warrior who considered Communism as an evil creed and that those who chose to be non-aligned as real enemies of the West. His doctrine that those who were not with the US were against the US had forced many developing countries to throw their lot with the Western bloc but Nehru viewed all these developments as having the potential for the revival of colonialism in a new form. Through his powerful advocacy of non-alignment he succeeded in persuading many developing countries to take an independent stand whenever issues of the Cold War raised difficult choices for them to make. It was because of this bold stand that he earned the encomium from Marshal Tito of Yugoslavia 'as the expression of human conscience'.

Nehru was more knowledgeable on foreign affairs than any of the civil servants working under him in the Ministry of External Affairs or India's diplomats in various countries. In fact he played a very important role in training the early groups of officers working in the Ministry of External Affairs at that time. They used to tell me that Nehru often dictated the replies to be sent to various cables received in the Ministry from our embassies asking for instructions from Delhi. Instead of waiting for drafts from below, Nehru himself would send to the concerned officers the texts of the letters, etc., to be issued by them. This was, indeed, excellent training for officers.

Jawaharlal had made significant contributions through his speeches and suggestions at the conferences of Commonwealth Heads of governments in the transformation of the old 'British Commonwealth' into the present 'Commonwealth of Nations'. There were several controversial issues like the position of the British sovereign in the Commonwealth, but Nehru had often provided solutions acceptable to all members making it possible for the Commonwealth to function without even a semblance of subordination to the crown in Britain.

Even though the record of Jawaharlal Nehru as Foreign Minister was an outstanding success, there were some instances where the stand taken by him had led to a lot of severe criticism both within India and from outside. The most important was his hesitation in declaring as wrong the action of the Soviet Union in putting down in a most repressive manner the rebellion in Hungary against Soviet domination in 1958. The critics of Nehru were quick to point out that he had been one of the harshest critics of Britain and France when they used their military might against Egypt when Nasser nationalized the Suez Canal. After a few weeks of sitting on the fence Nehru had come out with a statement supporting the aspirations of the people of Hungary for freedom, but it was too late and India's prestige in the world had suffered a severe beating. Even today it is difficult to explain why Nehru adopted different standards in the case of the Suez Canal and Hungary. It remains a blot on the otherwise unblemished record of Nehru's conduct of his country's foreign relations.

MODERNIZATION OF INDIA

One of the first steps taken by the Nehru government was the enactment of the Industrial Development and Regulation Act of 1951. This Act contributed later to some extent to what came to be condemned by his critics as the 'licence and permit raj'. The Act was intended among other things to preserve the limited resources, particularly of foreign exchange for imports, which were considered most essential for the development of the economy. Using this Act the government monitored the availability of goods and services indigenously produced in order to prevent the production of non-essential goods. While the Act was well intentioned its practical application led to widespread corruption and avoidable delays in the industrialization programmes of the country. It also created a new privileged group of monopolists who conveniently used the provisions of the Act to prevent competition to their products.

The second Industrial Policy resolution of 1956, marked a major step for the stimulation of industrial production and making the country self-sufficient in most consumer products and a substantial segment of capital goods. One of the greatest achievements of this period was the special programmes of assistance launched by the government to traditional industries which had high potential for employment and the development of backward areas, particularly rural areas. Such programmes included special assistance to handicrafts, handlooms, sericulture, village industries, modern small-scale industries, coir, rubber, etc. Separate organizations or Boards were established with liberal financial assistance for helping these sectors to overcome their handicaps and acquire competitive strength in the modern market.

Jawaharlal's attention had simultaneously turned to social reforms. Even though untouchability had been abolished under the Constitution, Indian society continued to be plagued by gross disparities and inequalities. In spite of the spread of education, women continued to endure several handicaps. Jawaharlal firmly believed that without radical changes in the status of women, they would always remain the exploited and disadvantaged class in the society. However, when he introduced the Hindu Code Bill aimed at removing some of the disabilities of women, he had to face strong opposition from the conservative sections in the Hindu society including some of the leading figures in the Congress party. Nehru persisted with his efforts, but it took six years to pass the two most important measures, namely, the Hindu Succession Act 1955 which gave women equal rights with men in the matter of succession and holding of property, and the Hindu Marriage Act 1956 which gave monogamy a legal basis and provided for divorce with alimony and maintenance.

The series of measures which Nehru introduced for social, economic and educational reforms in India had created tremendous enthusiasm, particularly among the younger generation and strengthened the confidence of the youth that India would emerge as a modern nation under Jawaharlal's leadership in a short time. The fact that there was not even a whisper of doubt about the highest standards of integrity and fairness maintained by the prime minister became an additional factor for his high reputation. However, by the beginning of the 1960s the world appeared to have changed for the people of India because of the aggression mounted on an unsuspecting nation by China whose cause it had been championing in international forums with great sincerity. A sense of betrayal had seized the people.

The Nehru Era, Phase III: 1961–4

During the last phase of his life Nehru again won a massive mandate of the people through the general elections of 1961. The Congress party led by Nehru won 361 seats in the Lok Sabha disproving all theories of anti-incumbency in Indian elections. In spite of the reassuring support of the people of India, 1961–4 turned out to be the most disappointing and unhappy phase personally for Nehru. Mao Tse-Tung had come to power in China in October 1949 and from the very beginning of the Communist regime it became clear to all observers of China that it did not have friendly designs with regard to India.

Soon after taking over power, the Communist regime announced that Tibet was an integral part of China and that China was determined to assert its authority over Tibet. Mao did not waste any time in ordering the march of his troops into Tibet and by October 1950 the Chinese army had taken control of Tibet. India had historically several rights in Tibet, but Beijing made it clear that it would not recognize any of them. India protested against China's takeover of Tibet by force and warned China that it would endanger India's efforts to get recognition for Mao's government and its admission to the United Nations. Beijing ignored these warnings, asserting that Tibet was its domestic matter.

After the occupation of Tibet, the Chinese government continued to behave as if nothing significant had happened to weaken its friendly relations with India. Chou En-Lai signed the Panchsheel agreement with Jawaharlal in 1954. In 1955, he attended the Bandung Conference of the Afro-Asian countries, using that opportunity to project a friendly face of China to the countries of Asia and Africa. However, China was quietly preparing for its war against India, the main objective of which was, besides territorial gains, to reduce India's importance and influence among the developing countries and to project China's status as the unchallenged super power in Asia.

Jawaharlal's visit to China in October 1954, was cleverly used by the Chinese to project that it valued its friendship with India and further to show that it had high regard for Jawaharlal as a great leader. About a million people had turned up on the 12-mile route from the airport to give Jawaharlal a grand welcome. Chou En Lai and Jawaharlal travelled together in an open car, doing away with for the only time for China, bullet-proof cars normally used by it for security reasons. In spite of China's professed keenness for maintaining friendly relations with India, China had repudiated the McMahon Line dubbing it as imperialist Britain's cartographic aggression over Chinese territory. India had taken the stand that the sanctity of the McMahon Line cannot be challenged. The Chinese through various statements had made Jawaharlal believe that they considered the difference of opinion on the McMahon Line only as an issue which could easily be settled by negotiations, but it had in the meanwhile been building roads and establishing military posts as part of its larger scheme of inflicting a humiliating defeat on an unsuspecting and unprepared India.

In 1959, the Dalai Lama along with several thousands of his followers escaped into India and India gave them asylum. This became a cause for China to accuse India of an unfriendly act towards China. By the beginning of 1961, China started questioning the legitimacy of Kashmir as a part of India in clear demonstration of its support for Pakistan. Jawaharlal during this period had sincerely believed that in spite of unfriendly noises on certain issues from China, that country would never go to the extent of launching a war on India. He thought that the worst thing China could do, would be to create minor skirmishes at the border in order to apply pressure on India on the boundary issue. No serious steps, therefore, were taken by Jawaharlal to improve the military capabilities of the Indian army for defending India's borders with China. In fact the allegation against India's Defence Minister V.K. Krishna Menon was that he never believed that China would go in for a war and had even converted some of the military factories into units for production of pressure cookers and other such consumer goods rather than the military hardware which the army badly needed for defence.

By September 1962, Chinese troops, well trained and equipped for warfare in high-altitude regions had crossed the McMahon Line at several points forcing the totally unprepared Indian troops behind the posts it had occupied. In the full-scale war which China unleashed India suffered the most humiliating defeat in its history. The victorious Chinese declared ceasefire on 21 November 1962, but retained 2500 square miles of Indian territory in the Eastern sector. None of Nehru's friends in the non-aligned camp came to India's defence even through statements of support. In fact both Tito and Nasser, great friends of Nehru, chose to practice non-alignment even in the face of aggression that India was experiencing! The only offer of support extended to India in this hour of need was from the Western bloc led by the US, though it has been argued that it might have had its own reasons for doing it. At any rate the war was over and there was no need for any active engagement with the Chinese with help from outside. Indian public opinion was outraged at the humiliation suffered by the country and Krishna Menon became the main target of criticism for this shameful failure. Nehru was a broken man by this time. A letter to Menon dated 28 October 1962, by Nehru reflects his mood at this time. He wrote, 'I do not know how I shall explain to Parliament, why we have been found lacking in equipment. It would not be much good shifting about the blame. The fact remains that we have been found lacking and there is an impression that we have approached these things in a somewhat amateurish way.'

Menon was forced to resign on 7 November. General Thapar, Chief of the Army staff, resigned on alleged health grounds and General Kaul who was in charge of the major part of the operations against China took premature retirement. Even though there was no serious demand that Nehru also should resign, several people in India were unhappy with the way the Chinese aggression had been handled by him.

Nehru's good health which in spite of his advancing years had always been a source of great happiness and confidence for the people, started declining and people noticed it with great concern. Those like me who had seen him at close range during this period in meetings with ministers and senior officers, had noticed a conspicuous puffiness on his face and a little unsteadiness in his gait. He was also sometimes seen dozing off in the middle of the meetings without fully following what was being discussed. Jawaharlal suffered a stroke while attending the meeting of the Congress at Bhubaneshwar on 16 January 1964, and the news of the poor state of his health was no longer a secret.

The last five months of Jawaharlal's Prime Ministership was a period of intense personal anguish for him because of the perfidy of the Chinese aggression on India. His agony was compounded by his own ill health. Because of his poor health, he could not travel around the country and explain how he had been misled by the Chinese leaders who he had trusted.

Jawaharlal held a Press Conference at Delhi on 20 May 1964, during which the members of the media clearly noticed the poor state of his health. One of the last questions thrown at him at this conference was why he was delaying to settle the question of succession. In reply he had said, 'My life is not going to end so soon'. But, alas, it was to end very soon.

Jawaharlal went off to Dehradun along with Indira Gandhi for a holiday, but on 26 May 1964, his daughter noticed further deterioration in his health and they returned to Delhi that evening. That night he worked as usual clearing all the files on his desk before retiring to sleep. At 6.25 on the morning of 27 May 1964, Jawaharlal Nehru was no more.

The end of Jawaharlal's life marked the end of a glorious era in Indian history. As M.J. Akbar in his brilliant biography of Jawaharlal has stated, 'The magic of his genius had created industry in the plains in central India, built dams in the hills from which rivers tumble into the fields, brought presidents and prime ministers to Delhi's door, from Khrushchev to Eisenhower, and sent the armies of India to keep peace in lands as distant as Korea and Congo and Gaza.' I would like to add that above all, the magic of his genius had won for him the genuine love and respect of millions of common people in India to a measure which few political leaders in the history of any country would have received.

There have been great administrators in history, but not all of them were also good human beings in an ethical sense. There have been good men at the helm of affairs in several countries, but not all of them were great administrators. There have been only a few in history who were both great administrators and good human beings. Jawaharlal Nehru was one of them.

KARAN SINGH

2

The Nehru Years

If 1920 to 1945 could be called the Gandhi Era, then 1947 to 1964 is, undoubtedly, the Nehru Era. This is not to be considered as, in any way, denigrating the galaxy of remarkable figures that were either contemporary or senior to Jawaharlal Nehru. Men like Sardar Vallabhbhai Patel, Maulana Azad, Rajendra Prasad, C.R. Rajagopalachari were all senior to Jawaharlal in age and in the Indian National Congress. They were strong provincial leaders also. Nonetheless, it is true that Jawaharlal was the predominant figure in that period. He left an indelible impact on almost every aspect of our public life.

I had the privilege of a very close association with him. In fact, I looked upon him as my political guru. I am not sure whether you have seen my correspondence with Jawaharlal Nehru, *Jammu and Kashmir: 1949–64*. It contains our correspondence with each other over a fifteen-year period. You will notice that each of his letters begins with 'My dear Tiger', because that was my pet name. My witness to the Nehruvian years is already encapsulated in this volume. I was a witness to and also a participant of those Nehru years. Here, I will try and mention some of the main events of that era in which Jawaharlal Nehru played such a major role. Each one of them could be expanded into a whole series of lectures.

Partition

The first point of discussion should be the Partition. The partition process, by 1946, had become irreversible, although Gandhiji and some members of the Congress held on to the very end. My own view is that, with the rejection of the Cripps Mission proposals, the partition of the country had virtually become inevitable. Sri Aurobindo, wrote a letter to the Congress in 1942, urging them to accept the Cripps Mission proposals because that was, as he put it, 'the last opportunity to save India's unity'. As it turned out, not only did Gandhiji and the Congress not accept the proposals, they decided to launch the Quit India Movement. As a result, all the Congressmen were thrown into jail and Jinnah emerged as the sole supporter and loyal servant of the British Empire. There was a last minute effort by the Cabinet Mission, led by Lord Pethick-Lawrence to avoid Partition. Thousands of people were being butchered on the streets of Calcutta (now Kolkata). Communal riots broke out all over the country. Mountbatten came in at just the right juncture. The whole history suddenly went fast forward. Before anybody knew what was happening, Independence was upon us. There is a moot question as to whether the Partition could have been prevented or not. The Partition was accompanied by the most terrible slaughter from both sides and one of the largest mass migrations in history. Doomsayers said that Indian freedom will never last; it will fail because of centuries of conflict. But Nehru could lead India through the birth pangs of a new nation. Let us never forget that the triumph of Independence was accompanied by the tragedy of the Partition. Everybody talks about our non-violent freedom struggle. But the violence that we committed upon each other also needs to be remembered. We need to remember that we paid in full the price for our freedom. We may not have had any violence against the British and that was a remarkable thing. Gandhiji's principles have been emulated around the world by Nelson Mandela, Martin Luther King, and others. But I have to point out as a witness to history, the terrible situation that prevailed at that time. Millions of Punjabis came with only the shirts on their backs.

They have today built Delhi into the city that it is through sheer hard work and grit. The same happened on the eastern border.

The new government—Jawaharlal Nehru, aided very ably by Sardar Patel, met the tremendous challenge. They proved the prophets of doom wrong. 'The tryst with destiny', that Jawaharlal spoke so eloquently about in the Constituent Assembly on the midnight of the 14–15 August 1947, that tryst was kept after a very heavy price was paid. Nonetheless, for the first time perhaps, India emerged as a democratic sovereign nation. That transition itself was a very major achievement. Had Jawaharlal Nehru passed away at that time, even then it would have been a tremendous achievement. But that was only the beginning. The Partition and the stabilization of India after the Partition was the first major challenge.

Framing of the Constitution

The second major challenge at that time was the framing and the adoption of our Constitution. Our Constitution emerged from two factors. There was the Government of India Act 1935 that gave, as it were, a constitutional framework. But the ideological, democratic, republican, and socialist inputs were the result of the work of the framers of the Constitution, where the scholarly Dr Rajendra Prasad presided, where Dr Babasahab Ambedkar headed the Drafting Committee which had such notables as Sir B.N. Rao, T.T. Krishnamachari and others, and where the influence and ideology of Jawaharlal Nehru was very strong and important. On every issue, it was his influence that tilted the scales and, not only the Fundamental Rights which were well accepted but the Directive Principles of State Policy, particularly, reflected Jawaharlal Nehru's ideology and vision. There were some things that were not justifiable at that time but were desirable goals. Panditji was an ideologue in the best sense of the term. His influence on the framing of the Constitution, although perhaps not so visible and dramatic as his other achievements, nonetheless needs to be recorded. For example, the first few amendments to the Constitution, particularly the first one which expedited and facilitated land reforms should be noted. According to the Fundamental Rights, one would have to pay the market price for any land that one took over. That would not have been possible as it meant paying large sums of money to the land owners which India did not have.

So the first amendment to the Constitution was to enable land reforms to take place without having to pay market rent. Jawaharlal Nehru was passionately committed to democratic socialism.

Democracy is the longer road to development. China took the shorter road. They paid a horrible price. Millions have perished under Communist regimes. Under Stalin, millions were starved to death. Under Mao, millions of Chinese perished. Today they are, no doubt, ahead of us. But we have tried to develop in a democratic way. It is very impressive to see what the Chinese have achieved. Their infrastructure, their roads, their bridges, their airports, their buildings are far, far ahead of us. We should also be able to catch up with them provided we can deliver. When I was in China, I read a comment by an American futurologist who said that it was China, not India that would emerge as the next superpower. India has been talking about a new airport for the last 30 years, whereas China has been building an airport of international standards every 13 months.

Integration of Indian States

The third important point is the integration of Indian states. That, of course, was the main task of Sardar Patel. He was ably assisted by V.P. Menon. Nowhere in world history will one find a parallel where hundreds of princely states and feudal principalities voluntarily surrendered their territories to form part of a larger union. It was an extraordinary feat. The princes also deserve some credit for being patriotic. Let us not forget that it was Jawaharlal Nehru who was the Prime Minister at the time. Although he left the integration of states largely to Sardar Patel, he was the person who presided over it. The map of India during the British period was a patchwork quilt. There were a total of about four to five hundred principalities scattered all over. Some of them went to Pakistan. Most of them were in India. To convert that into one nation was a very big task. There were problems in Hyderabad and Junagadh. The issue of my home state, Jammu and Kashmir is an important one. It was a rather difficult special case. All the main rivers of the state flowed into Pakistan. Many of the younger generation today assume that Jammu and Kashmir could have automatically become a part of India. But there was no such assumption then. In fact, there could have been a reverse assumption. But it so happened that my father (Maharaja Hari Singh), for some reason did not make up his mind by 15 August 1947. Then he tried to have a standstill agreement. Then, of course, there was a tribal invasion in October 1947. It forced him to accede and the rest is history. There it was Jawaharlal Nehru's own particular question. He took a lot of interest in it. A lot of people blamed him for that. But if you look at it from his point of view, he perhaps thought that an 80 per cent Muslim majority state voluntarily joining the Indian union would greatly strengthen the secular foundations of India. Pakistan was clearly a Muslim state and they made no secret of it. It was an Islamic republic. But not only did the Constitution-makers in India not create a Hindu republic, they bent over backwards to provide a secular state and to give special protection to minorities. So, I think, Jammu and Kashmir, in some ways, became an ideological test case. Pakistan felt that since it was a Muslim majority state, it should join Pakistan under the scheme of the Partition. Jawaharlal Nehru disagreed and was of the opinion that the state had its own decision. There was no reason why a Muslim majority state should not join India. In reply to my father's letter about the Instrument of Accession, Lord Mountbatten, with Jawaharlal Nehru's approval, put in the fateful words, 'When normalcy is restored, we will try and ascertain the wishes of the people'. The rest is history, as they say. People talk about plebiscite. The first prerequisite of the plebiscite was that Pakistan was to totally withdraw from the state. But I am not going into the minutiae of the Jammu and Kashmir problem. Hundreds of books have been written on it. It is true that Jawaharlal was perhaps over-insistent upon power being handed over to Sheikh Abdullah immediately. He also perhaps did not realize that although Sheikh Abdullah was the charismatic leader of the Kashmiris, it was not about Kashmir alone. It was about Jammu and Kashmir. Even today when people refer to the Kashmir issue, they do not realize that there is no such state as Kashmir. There never was a state named Kashmir. The state built up by my forefathers and ruled by my father was the state of Jammu and Kashmir which stretched from the plains of the Punjab right into the steppes of Central Asia and from the Punjabi areas of Mirpur all the way into the heart of Tibet. It was a multi-regional, multi-ethnic, multi-geographical, multi-religious, and multi-linguistic state. Through that major lack of proper understanding, it was assumed that Sheikh Abdullah was the leader of Jammu and Kashmir. He was, no doubt, the leader of the Kashmiris. He transformed the Kashmiris from a downtrodden bunch of people into a self-confident community. But he was never able to carry the rest of the state with him. That ultimately led to his fall. It is a long story. But it remained with Jawaharlal Nehru for the whole of his life. One of the last things that Panditji did was to send Sheikh Abdullah to Pakistan, Pakistan-occupied Kashmir, and Muzaffarabad in order to try and bring about some kind of an agreed solution. It was when Sheikh Abdullah was speaking in Muzaffarabad that somebody handed him a note saying that Jawaharlal Nehru was no more. Of course, he broke down as he was very closely and emotionally bound to Panditji. So, from the very first day right until the end, the Jammu and Kashmir affair, particularly the Kashmir matter, was something that hung heavily on Jawaharlal Nehru's shoulders.

Linguistic States

The formation of linguistic states after the achievement of freedom was part of the manifesto of the Congress and of Gandhiji's movement. Linguistic reorganization of India was done by the three-member 1953 States' Reorganization Commission headed by Justice Sayyid Fazal Ali with, if I remember correctly, Pandit Hridaynath Kunzru and Sardar K.M. Panikkar. They travelled all over the country and brought out the States' Reorganization Commission report. Unfortunately, it stopped at the Jammu and Kashmir border. Jammu and Kashmir was never considered because it had a separate situation. For the first time, there was a rationalization of the boundaries in the interiors of India. This was a major thing. Panditji had his own views; for example, he was against Bombay being partitioned. But there is a logic to it. The attempt to linguistically reorganize states did not stop at the formation of Maharashtra and Gujarat. Panditji, I must say, was somewhat partial to Uttar Pradesh (UP). Sardar K.M. Panikkar had said at that time that UP should be divided into three states because, according to him, it was too big a state. But in those days all the leadership came from UP. So for them any talk of dividing UP was sacrilege. Today, almost 60 years later, Mayawati has once again made the same demand to divide UP into three parts. This is how history repeats itself. Linguistic states were required for effective federalism. Reorganization was required as Marathwada went into Maharashtra, Telengana went into

Andhra Pradesh and Gulbarga went into Karnataka. All the state borders were redrawn on a rational basis. That was a very important development at that time over which Pandit Nehru presided.

Planning

Panditji was enamoured of the Soviet Five-Year Plan system. He realized, of course, that the Soviet model of a totally controlled economy would not work in India. Nonetheless, he introduced the Five-Year plans. Of course, J.R.D. Tata and others had made the Bombay Plan earlier. At that time, the public sector was to lead the economy. Perhaps it was wise, because if we had not, at that time, made necessary investments in heavy industry, steel, coal, and railways, the infrastructure for today's liberalization would not have been there. India had a mixed economy. The Five-Year plans still continue. We are into the 11th Five-Year Plan now.

Community Development

Nehru was also keen on community development. He set up the Ministry for Community Development. Panditji wanted a participatory democracy, a democracy in which the people would not simply look up to the government but be active participants in the process of development. Unfortunately, that never actually took off. It was only half a century later when Rajiv Gandhi came through with the Panchayati Raj Institutions Act that an attempt was again made to involve local participation. Until the people are involved in the developmental process, adequate development can never be achieved. That is where the vision of Jawaharlal Nehru, although it was not fulfilled at the time, is still valid and today, unprecedented sums of money have been allotted for poverty alleviation programmes, whether it is the Bharatiya Grameen Rozgar Yojana or the Sarvashiksha Abhiyaan, whether it is Bharat Nirmaan, the Urban Renewal Mission, or the Midday Meals Programme. But are they being delivered? The money can be granted by the Government of India. It is for the state governments and for the zilla parishads and the panchayats to deliver the money. Unless that happens, our developmental process will never really succeed. A lot of money gets siphoned off through corruption and inefficiency. This was something that Jawaharlal Nehru foresaw.

Science and Technology

Jawaharlal Nehru was very keen on the development of science and technology. He laid the foundation for the Indian Institutes of Technology, as a result of which, today India is recognized around the world for its information technology (IT) capabilities. Nehru was a votary of science and he constantly stressed that science and technology were the only mechanisms whereby the centuries-old poverty could be alleviated. Poverty alleviation was and will remain the major challenge before us. Application of science and technology in agriculture, industry, and atomic energy was very important in the eyes of Nehru. So he took a lot of interest in that. He took along eminent scientists like Homi Bhabha, Vikram Sarabhai, Shanti Swaroop Bhatnagar, and Homi Sethna, and others who were involved in this whole process of institutionalizing science and technology in the country. I think that must be counted as one of the major achievements of Panditji's mission. He never really paid any attention to the population problem. He always said that development would take care of that. Development has not taken care of it. My own view is that the tripling of our population over the last sixty years has diluted much of the gains of our economic development. When we are still adding one Australia every year to our population, from where are we going to get the jobs, the food, the houses for the people of the country? This was the question which Nehru used to brush aside. He was often misled by his advisers. He often chose wrong advisers. For example, in the debacle of 1962, I think, clearly Krishna Menon, although he was a brilliant man and a great freedom fighter, misled Jawaharlal Nehru on the forward policy regarding China. It is not as if Jawaharlal Nehru was without his faults. He did suffer a lack of judgement in many areas. But overall, his performance must be looked upon as absolutely outstanding.

Foreign Policy

Jawaharlal Nehru remained, till the end of his life, his own Foreign Minister. He never appointed a Cabinet Minister for Foreign Affairs because he was greatly interested in and fascinated by foreign affairs. Even before the Independence Movement, he travelled a lot and guided our foreign policy. I met President Nasser, President Tito, and Archbishop Makarios at Teen

Murti House. All these people used to flock there. It became the centre of the anti-colonial movement around the world. India's freedom breached the main citadels of the colonial rule. If the beginning of the colonial rule can be dated back to 1498 when Vasco de Gama landed in Goa, the end of the colonial rule began in 1947. Within ten years dozens of nations had become free. Jawaharlal Nehru was in the forefront in the Asian Relations Conference, the Bandung Conference and the Non-Aligned Movement. Quite possibly, he saved the world from yet another conflagration over the Cold War. Nehru said that India had not become free to join some other camp. He thus developed an alternative model, which, at that time, was extremely significant for world peace. At that time, in those crucial and critical years, after the end of the Second World War up till the end of the Cold War, the Non-Aligned Movement played a very important role. I think that Jawaharlal Nehru's contribution to world peace—the anti-colonial movement, his opposition to apartheid in South Africa, his opposition to the Suez attack by the UK—all of these will go down in history as a very major contribution at that time. Jawaharlal Nehru was not only an Indian leader. He was a world leader in the best sense of the term. He never tried to develop India's hegemony over anybody else. However, he was quite unapologetic that India was the centre for the anti-colonial movement. He tried wherever possible, to assist, morally or materially, the anti-colonial movements around the world.

To sum up, therefore, in the crucial years between 1947 and 1964, Jawaharlal Nehru bestrode this nation like a colossus. It is fitting that this can be called the 'Nehruvian Era'. If Mahatma Gandhi is rightly called the Father of the Indian Nation, then Jawaharlal Nehru could rightly be called the Father of the Indian State.

SUBHASH KASHYAP

3

Jawaharlal Nehru

From Far and Near—Some Recollections

Nehru was one of the finest and the greatest human beings who strode this world like a colossus and whose name, thoughts, and deeds thrilled and inspired me from my early childhood. Not many witnesses to the history of the Nehru era of Indian history are left on the scene. Soon there will be hardly anyone who has seen the titans like Nehru, Patel, Gandhi, Prasad, Ambedkar, and others in flesh and blood. Those who had met them, talked to them, worked with them would be rarer to find.

I must begin by mentioning two constraints. First, in all such undertakings involving personal reminiscences, there is always a danger of the human temptation of the narrator to go autobiographical, talk more about oneself and seek to parade one's nearness to the great men in the subconscious hope of shining a little in their reflected glory. In the process, a sense of balance and objectivity may be sacrificed for ego satisfaction. One needs to be very cautious and exercise all the necessary self-restraint. Second, Nehru's role in the framing and working of the Constitution of India and shaping the history of the Parliament during the first seventeen crucial years have already been discussed by me in depth in the six books in the field of Nehruvian studies. The theme of Nehru and the Constitution was again covered in my contribution to the Nehru Centenary volume. Nehru and the Parliament was the topic of my last lecture here at the Nehru Centre and it appears in the volume *Nehru Revisited*. But in all these works, even in matters to which I was personally privy, I have never used the first person. I find it difficult and uncomfortable now to revisit those areas in the format of personal reminiscences. I shall, therefore, largely leave these matters out. I must also clarify, at the very outset, that my recollections of Nehru are only those of a child who was privileged to see him from near; of a student activist who had a few occasions to meet him, talk to him, and even preside at one large gathering of students at Allahabad University addressed by him and; and lastly of a young parliamentary officer in Delhi who saw him function in the Parliament during 1953–64. I can claim no closeness or special relationship with Nehru. I was only 35 years when he left us. Most of the time, I had occasion to see him from a distance. But there were proud moments when I got the opportunity to get nearer, exchange some words, and feel his charisma.

Since my father and the family in a small town in western Uttar Pradesh (UP) were active in the national struggle for freedom, the name 'Jawaharlal Nehru' echoed in our house and I must have first heard it in my mother's womb and in the cradle. My father had worked with Pandit Motilal Nehru and later, closely with Jawaharlal Nehru. Allahabad, then the all India headquarters of the Congress, and Swaraj Bhavan was like a second home to him. My father used to bring back and narrate many stories about the Nehrus—Motilal Nehru's aristocratic lifestyle, his wardrobe, his transformation to thick khadi, his dressing habits, his old servant, Anand Bhavan, and so on. He dismissed the stories of the Nehru clothes being washed in Paris, etc. as being false. He, however, used to tell us that it was Jawaharlal Nehru who dragged Motilal Nehru into politics. My own first glimpse of Uncle Nehru was only sometime in the year 1937. He had come to our hometown to address a large public gathering in connection with the Legislative Assembly polls. Nehru was taken out in a large procession. My mother along with the ladies and children of our house had assembled and they were waiting at the main entrance of the house which fell, almost by design, on the procession route. The procession stopped in front of our house and Nehru offered to walk in. My mother did some *arati* and presented a bag containing the donations collected for the Congress fund. I was a child but cannot forget that I felt like having seen the most handsome man. He was wearing a white khadi dhoti, kurta, Gandhi cap, and a waistcoat which had come to be called 'Jawahar vascat'. The procession ended at the venue of the public meeting in front of the municipal hall. When a Congress worker tried to help Nehru to take off his Peshawari shoes before sitting on the dais floor, Nehru brushed him aside and scolded him for his slavish mentality. Although it was supposed to be an election rally, Nehru talked about the world, Europe, etc. One couplet that he recited and which I still remember ran something like this:

Hamne manzilein teh ki hain kuchh is tarah
Hum chale. Chal kar gire. Gir kar uthe. Utth kar chale.

The people, mostly villagers, it seems to me in retrospect, only looked at his face and felt enchanted. In any case, the ordinary folks present were then not part of the limited electorate. Before the meeting ended, my father and a couple of other workers sat in a jeep to rush as an advance party for the venue of the next meeting which was some miles away in the interior. I was allowed to go along. We waited on the roadside. When Nehru's cavalcade appeared, my father stood in the middle of the road and waved to the cars to stop. Nehru's programme was already running behind schedule and, apparently he had no idea of this engagement on the way. He was angry and expressed his annoyance to my father. But soon he cooled down when my father too very firmly told him that his time was not his own and belonged to the ordinary village people who had been waiting for him for hours. For reaching the venue of the meeting, we had to walk for a few minutes which Nehru did most sportingly. I remember that he walked very fast and it was not easy for others to keep pace with him. When we were walking through the fields, a simple villager rushed towards him and presented some sugarcane to him. Nehru, taken by the loving gesture, wanted to chew the sugarcane and he was helped to taste a bit of it.

After being involved in the 1942 Quit India Movement and before entering college I had finished reading Nehru's autobiography in Hindi, *Meri Kahaani*, *Letters from a Father to His Daughter*, also in Hindi *Pita Ke Patra Putri Ke Naam*, and *Glimpses of World History* in English. His autobiography was almost a contemporary history of India. The most touching and poignant passages for me were those devoted to his loving wife, Kamala Nehru who he had lost recently and to whose memory the book was dedicated. Nehru emerges as being somewhat remorseful for not having been adequately supportive and appreciative of his devoted life companion. As a student at Meerut College, I was active in the Students' Congress and strongly opposed to the Communist counterpart, the Students' Federation. The Students' Congress worked in close collaboration with the District Congress leaders. Choudhary Charan Singh was the District Congress Committee president. Elections to the Central Legislative Assembly and the provincial Assemblies were scheduled for 1945–6. When Nehru was to visit Meerut, in the later part of 1945, we had several organizational meetings at Choudhary Charan Singh's house. I remember that Nehru arrived by road very late in the night. He was wearing a black sherwani and as he moved past the parade of college girls to welcome him, he kept putting his hands in the sherwani pockets and picking up a few grams (*chanas*) and munching them. Suddenly, he stopped and started admonishing the organizers for keeping the girl volunteers waiting for such late hours in the night. Like a traditional Indian father, he then told the girls not to stay out so late in the night.

Next morning, the tour to the villages had to commence. We of the Students' Congress team moved ahead of the leaders. As the road connectivity was poor I once again saw Nehru walking on his feet to reach the meeting venue. My father had given me a Kodak box camera on my birthday, which I was carrying. In the midst of the fields, on some impulse, I started aiming the camera at Nehru for his photograph. He looked at me, smiled and gave me my first lessons in the art of photography. I was aiming with the sun in front. Nehru said that should never be done. The sun should always be behind. He most graciously stood under a tree, posed for me, and then asked me to take the picture. I still treasure the photograph as a proud possession and it forms part of a valuable memorabilia. Having got the photo, I was encouraged to seek another favour. I extended towards him a newly purchased autograph book and requested him for his autograph. Nehru said, 'You also need autographs? Someday, you should be giving them.' I did not understand what he meant. But he was angry and threw away my autograph book. I never had an autograph book before that and never kept one later.

I cannot forget another incident during the short walk through the fields. A rustic boy, about 9–10 years old, was walking with us. I noticed that Nehruji once instinctively came close to affectionately putting his hands on the boy's head but then resisted. Obviously, he had noticed that the boy's head was dirty and dusty. It seemed to illustrate the contradictions between Nehru's socialistic instincts and his aristocratic upbringing. That day the tour ended at a large meeting at Ghaziabad near Delhi. The crowd, in its enthusiasm, was boisterous and unruly. Everyone was trying to surge forward to have a better view of their beloved leader. When the volunteers failed to control the mob, Nehru jumped from the podium over the heads of the jostling crowd. Soon, surprisingly, there was order. This had, in fact, become a well-tried Nehru strategy for crowd management. The meeting was followed by tea at which prominent citizens including industrialists, old landlords, Congress leaders, etc. were present. In the midst of the party, everybody was taken aback when Nehru stood up, put his hands on the table and literally jumped to the other side. He was, perhaps, tired after the long day. He was, perhaps, fed up with the formal atmosphere at the party or perhaps, the playful child in Nehru was again seeking expression. Sometimes, very small incidents like these which usually go unnoticed throw valuable light on a man's inner personality.

Nehru was inspired by and felt invigorated in crowds, among the people. He was not a great orator, at least not in Hindi. Often, he spoke in halting, rambling Hindi-Urdu. His style was that of a teacher, trying to explain things. While speaking, he was also thinking aloud with the audience. A constant refrain in his public speeches during the period was that great things were happening all over the globe while we were engaged in petty narrow squabbles. Events were moving very fast and, to keep pace, we also had to run. When Independence came, my father, a staunch Gandhian, decided to completely withdraw from politics. He thought that the work was over and what would follow would only be a fight for chairs. Nehru considered this to be a very narrow way of looking at things and he told him so. Directly and through Pandit Pant, he tried to persuade my father to remain active in the Congress. He thought that the real time to work for the nation had come only now. A tried and tested man should not desert the ship midway.

As an undergraduate student of the University of Allahabad during 1946–8, I had the pleasure of reading Nehru's latest book *The Discovery of India*. It made it very clear that Nehru was more of an English gentleman who had to discover India to feel proud of the great ancient heritage. The book contained a considerable repetition of facts from the *Glimpses of World History*. Otherwise, the two books could be considered world classics. Once, Nehru visited Allahabad University and addressed the students at the Senate Hall under the auspices of the University Union. Narain Dutt Tiwari was then the President of the Union. I happened to be the Publications Secretary. The meeting was followed by a get-together of the guests with the union executives. For me, it was a pleasure again to be admonished by Nehru and to learn some table manners from no less a person than the Prime Minister of India himself. I had peeled an orange before presenting it to Nehru. He said, '*Dekho tumko ek principle ki baat bataate hai. Kabhi kisiko phal chilkar nahi dena chahiye.*' He also admonished me on passing food across the table.

Once at Anand Bhavan, I saw Pamela Mountbatten sitting on the steps of the Bhavan and Nehru, while getting into the car, asking her, 'Pammi, are you not coming?' He used to call her Pammi. As was well-known, Nehru was a little temperamental and could get really upset and angry. But he usually cooled down fast. I remember how he was annoyed with a student on the university campus who was walking ahead of him and was repeatedly taking photographs with an expensive camera. Nehru snatched the camera and threw it away. The student, a little lame, quickly walked away limping and muttering, 'If the Prime Minister has such a temper, God save the country.' Soon thereafter, the boy was invited to Anand Bhavan and Nehru offered him a nice, new camera. It is another matter that the proud student did not accept it.

During 1949–50, when I was president of the Allahabad University Union and Executive Chairman of what was then called the All India Universities Students' Organization, we decided to convene an Asian University Students' Conference to discuss common problems, need for mutual co-operation to safeguard the future of the young nations in Asia, and the role expected of the educated youth in Asian countries. For some reasons best known to them, the government did not want that Conference to take place at that time. But, in our youthfulness, we persisted and continued writing to the Government of UP and Government of India hoping that either they would allow it or they should openly come forward to disallow or ban it. I was residing at a university hostel and, one fine morning, there was a knock at my door. When I opened the door, to my great astonishment and embarrassment, I found Lal Bahadur Shastri, the then Police Minister of UP, standing outside with District Magistrate Bhargava and several others. I was told that Nehru wanted to see me at Anand Bhavan as soon as possible. I got ready quickly and reached Anand Bhavan. But he had just left for the airport. At the airport, Pandit Nehru was at his charming and endearing best. He said that he was coming to Allahabad again next month and wanted to address university and college students from all parts of the district. He asked me if the University Union could organize such a meeting under its auspices. Incidentally, I should mention that Nehru had been an honorary member of the Allahabad University Union for several years. Naturally, well aware of the geography and logistics of the university campus, Nehru himself indicated to me the details of where the dais should be built, and so on. He also said that he wanted this meeting to be restricted, as far as possible, to university level students, and it should not become a public meeting. This, he said, could be done by clearly announcing that the prime minister would be speaking in English. Accordingly, all the colleges in the district were informed, invited, and told that the prime minister would speak in English. Arrangements were made on the lines indicated.

On the appointed day, more than a lakh students turned up at the Muir College ground stadium site. Unfortunately, it started raining. But the crowds remained undisturbed and glued to their places even though fully drenched. We were all anxiously awaiting the arrival of Nehru. But Munshiji (as Nehru called Lal Bahadur Shastri) came instead of Nehru. He said that Panditji wanted to be sure that the students were still waiting. Obviously seeing the disciplined crowd of more than a lakh young boys and girls in his home town, waiting for him in the torrential rain, Nehru was in a very joyful mood. Seeing a large battery of mikes on the dais, he asked me why so many were needed. I referred to the news reports of successive failures of audio system in his previous meetings. He smiled at it. The then Vice Chancellor, Bhattacharya who was present on the dais tried to protect the prime minister from rain by holding an umbrella over his head. True to his style, Nehru brushed him aside saying that if the large crowd could stand in the rain, he too should do so. I welcomed Nehru with a few words in my poor English. Perhaps enthused by the huge crowd, Nehru started speaking in his well-known Hindustani. He referred to the debate that was then going on in the Constituent Assembly regarding the Devanagari vs. Arabic numerals. He also spoke about the upsurge in Asia and Africa, dying colonialism, and rising expectations from freedom and democracy. In my vote of thanks and concluding remarks, I explained to Panditji that the Union proceedings were always conducted in Hindi and that an exception had been made on that day on Nehruji's own instructions (which he had perhaps forgotten). On the upsurge in Asia and Africa, I referred to Nehru inaugurating the Asian Relations Conference and the eighteen-nation Conference in Indonesia. I said that the youth of Asia also wanted to meet. But the Asian University Students' Conference was not allowed by the Government. Nehru was a little upset. He took the microphone from me and intervened to say that he was informed that it was not opportune to hold the proposed conference at that time. But it could certainly be held at some future date. I was encouraged and made some efforts afterwards to retrieve the proposed conference. In my efforts, I met Chief Minister Pant at his Nainital residence and called on Prime Minister Nehru at his South Block office. Nothing much came out of the meetings. But I shall never forget the courtesy and consideration extended to me by Prime Minister Nehru. I was a mere student. But the Prime Minister talked to me and stood up to see me off till the door of his office room.

Later, when Nehru visited Allahabad, I had the honour to be invited to Anand Bhavan. Once I met him in the impressive first-floor study. The second time, before the 1951–2 elections to the Lok Sabha, it was a meeting of prominent citizens and workers in the large ground floor room. Prabhudutta Brahmachari was the powerful candidate pitted against Nehru.

I joined the Secretariat of the Lok Sabha (lower house of the Parliament) as an officer on the research side early during the First Lok Sabha. Although the selection was made by the Union Public Service Commission, the fact that I was till then a habitual khadi wearer, and the then Lok Sabha Secretary M.N. Kaul was from Allahabad, helped spread rumours that

I was brought to the Lok Sabha by Nehru. It had both advantages and disadvantages. Of course, it had no basis of any kind. Be that as it may, I had a long innings of over thirty-seven years in the Lok Sabha Secretariat. These included twelve years of Nehru's stay as the leader of the House and the prime minister. There was no occasion for me, at any time, to feel that Nehru ever recognized me by my family or Allahabad links. After all, I was only a junior officer.

When Nehru passed away in May 1964, I was working as In-charge of the five-volume study on the framing of India's Constitution. It was a project of the Indian Institute of Public Administration (IIPA) under the guidance of the Shiva Rao Committee. Nehru as Prime Minister, had taken keen and unfailing interest in the project from its commencement. His encouragement and assistance proved invaluable at every stage. On 6 August 1963, the Prime Minister had written to Shiva Rao that the work being done would be of enduring importance. When the project neared its completion, Nehru was requested to contribute a Foreword to it. Perhaps, this was one of the very last letters signed by him at Circuit House, Dehradun, on 24 May 1964. It was received by us only a few hours before the shocking news of his demise came. It said that he was sure that the study on which Shiva Rao and others were working would be very useful and that although he could not promise, he would try to send a Foreword later in the year.

While in the service of the Lok Sabha, I had the opportunity to see Nehru function in the House. Nehru was invariably present during the Question Hour almost every day and through all major debates. His presence in the House for long hours had a sobering effect on all other members in both sides of the House. I picked up from Prime Minister Nehru the habit of disposing off office files while sitting in the House and actively listening to the debates. As Secretary General for over seven years, I was able to dispose off a large number of files while sitting in the House. Nehru played the most outstanding role in building our parliamentary institutions and establishing healthy practices and precedents. The role of the Speaker was also important. But even he could not achieve much without the solid commitment and support from the prime minister and leader of the House. Nehru's relations with the Speaker and with all the members of the House, including those in the Opposition, were most cordial and admirable.

One does remember at least two occasions when Prime Minister Nehru clashed with Speaker Mavalankar. One was through correspondence on the issue of ordinances. Nehru, perhaps in an unguarded moment, said that the House should be adjourned early because the government wanted to issue some ordinances. Mavalankar took serious exception to it, saying that it would be a misuse of Article 123 of the Constitution. Nehru felt that it was entirely the prerogative of the government to decide when to advice adjournment of the House and when to issue ordinances. Mavalankar, on the other hand, said that while legally Nehru may be right, it was the height of impropriety to transfer legislative powers from the Parliament to the executive and Article 123 (ordinance-making power) was meant only for being used in extreme cases and rarely. Ultimately, a compromise was reached when Nehru continued to insist that it was entirely for the government to decide and that it had the power to issue ordinances when it liked. But he conceded that, with respect to Mavalankar's wisdom and advice, he would exercise restraint in the issue of ordinances and resort to them only when absolutely necessary.

The second time they clashed was when Nehru had made a statement and, after hearing other members, he wanted to make a second statement. The rules of Lok Sabha did not allow a second statement to be made by him. So Speaker Mavalankar disallowed it. Nehru was annoyed and failed to understand why he could not speak. But, ultimately, when Mavalankar was equally adamant, Nehru gracefully bowed to the Chair and sat down. The incident of the Speaker wanting to see the prime minister and the latter insisting that it is for the prime minister to come to the Speaker's chamber has often been cited by me and by others as one establishing high traditions of respect for parliamentary institutions. Nehru always found out the convenience of the Speaker and went to meet him at his chamber. This went a long way in establishing the supremacy and primacy of the legislature over the executive.

Nehru's regular visits to the House, his punctual and graceful entry with respectful bows to the Chair and to both sides of the House, even during his last days, are all parts of recorded history and have been described earlier. Several people have commented on how he would insist upon standing and speaking in the House, even when he was very ill. Even after being advised by the Speaker to remain seated, he would struggle to stand up to speak.

I recall that a brochure on 'Defence Matters in British Parliament' prepared by us could not be circulated as it was felt by some in the Government, that it would give wrong ideas to the members about their role and they would cite the position in the British Parliament and ask for similar information in India. But, Nehru personally was most anxious to share all the necessary information with the members. Debates on the international situation were eagerly looked forward to. So long as Nehru lived, in every session there used to be a motion moved by Nehru himself saying 'I move that the international situation be taken into consideration.' After Nehru, this has become history. When the word spread that the prime minister was going to speak, all of us crowded the galleries. I was witness to some momentous occasions like the debate on the nationalization of the Suez Canal. As part of my research duties, I prepared two studies on the subject. Apart from being made available to the members of the Parliament, a large number of copies of these studies were sent to the External Publicity Division of the External Affairs Ministry at their request for supply to Indian missions abroad. Krishna Menon took with him some copies of the brochure when he went on a negotiating and conflict resolution mission. Similarly, some other studies prepared by me on subjects like 'Military Alliances' and 'Panchsheel' were reported to have been warmly appreciated personally by the prime minister who spoke to the Speaker and suggested that such work must continue.

We, on the Research and Reference side, had started a new teleprinter service to keep the members informed of the latest news. Every few minutes, the teleprinter dispatches were checked and relevant items were displayed on a board prominently placed on the entrance of the ground floor library. One day, when I was checking the items displayed, I was taken aback on seeing Prime Minister Nehru standing by my side and asking me about the latest news. Obviously, those were very different days. We were witness to an era in democracy where the smallest man could find the greatest of men standing by his side. Once, Nehru needed some information most urgently with regard to a legislative matter. To save time, he himself walked into a Lok Sabha Secretariat branch asking for the information. Seeing the prime minister, all the staff were awe-struck and lost their nerve. It was unprecedented and most unexpected. The old Section Officer somehow collected his wits and requested Pandit Nehru with folded hands to please go and said: 'Sir, once you go, you will have the information in your hands within minutes.' Nehru smiled and walked out. We are unlikely ever to get another prime minister who can personally walk into a branch of the Secretariat asking the junior staff for urgent information.

Some developments in the House are indelibly etched in my memory. The integration of Goa had to be done forcibly because the Portuguese failed to respond to all gestures of friendliness. The much needed constitutional recognition was duly given in March 1962, when Goa was formally incorporated into the Indian Union. Moving the 12th Constitutional Amendment Bill on 14 March 1962, Nehru proudly proclaimed in the Lok Sabha that Indian Independence became complete only after the last vestige of Western imperialism was shown the way out with the contempt it deserved. Nehru's joy at this completion of Independence was natural. He said,

> The Bill means the end of an epoch and the beginning of another for Goa and for India. It has something of history attached to it. I feel that, for this House which has thought passionately about Goa in these many years, it is a matter of great satisfaction that the question has been settled and that an anachronism of history has been removed. The independence of India has become complete.

I have personally witnessed several debates in the Parliament. For example, the ruthless and brutal criticism by Lohia comparing the average daily income of an Indian and the daily expenditure on Nehru's dogs. Lohia had said, 'Hindustan ke aam aadami ki aamdani 25 paise roj hai aur in hajrat ke kutte ka roj ka kharcha 25 rupaye hai'. I remember Nehru sitting smilingly through all this. Then there were debates on science policy and industrial policy resolutions. Nehru intervened in the debate on Rukmini Arundale's bill on cruelty to animals. It was a private member's bill which Nehru accepted. For the last thirty years, not a single private member's bill has been accepted. There were fourteen private members' bills passed during the 1st, 2nd, 3rd, and 4th Lok Sabha but none thereafter. When a motion of no-confidence in his government was moved and discussed in the Lok Sabha, Nehru welcomed it as an opportunity.

Nehru would patiently sit through strong attacks on him and his government and, at the end, deliver his spirited reply. One remembers the firm handling of Kripalani's motion on General Thimayya and Nehru's declaration that in India civil authority would remain supreme.

Parliamentary historians shall always recall Nehru's strong response to disorderly conduct by some members during the President's address, giving a fitting reply to Kripalani's bitter and biting criticism during a debate on the budget, agreeing to refer M.O. Mathai's remarks to the Privileges Committee, welcoming valid and well-deserved criticism, accepting Ashok Mehta's criticism of the President's address, heated exchanges between Nehru and Shyama Prasad Mukherjee, full of fiery retorts, witty repartees and rejoinders, and accepting Rajaji's logic and the amendment moved by him even though Nehru had the majority with him. One can hardly visualize such things in the present-day houses of the Parliament.

Once, when Atal Bihari Vajpayee made an unsparing and frontal verbal attack on Nehru in the Lok Sabha, Nehru not only patiently listened to it but at an evening reception the same day, without any bitterness, told him, '*Aaj to aapne bada jabardast hamla kiya*'. When another member from Assam was in a furious mood attacking Nehru right and left on the floor of the House, Nehru was reported to have followed him into the lobby, placed his hand around the member's shoulders, and asked him how the work on the manuscript of his book was progressing.

Nehru once told the Lok Sabha:

Parliamentary democracy is a delicate plant and it is a measure of our own success that the plant has become sturdier during the last few years. We have faced difficulties and great problems and solved many of them. But many remain to be solved. If there are no problems, that is a sign of death. Only the dead have no problems. The living have problems and they grow fighting with problems and overcoming them. It is a sign of the growth of this nation that, not only do we solve problems but we create new problems to solve.

Incidentally, this statement has mightily influenced my thinking ever since it was made in the year 1957. I have often quoted it fully or in parts, sometimes appropriately attributing it to Nehru and at other times merely plagiarizing his ideas.

Speaking at a seminar on parliamentary democracy on 25 February 1956, Nehru said, 'Democracy is a means to an end. What is the end we aim at? I do not know if everybody will agree with me but I would say the end is the good life for the individual.' When the Communist Government in Kerala was found unable to control the law and order situation, President's rule was imposed on 30 July 1959. Chief Minister Namboodiripad had ignored

Nehru's advice to hold fresh elections. When the opposition accused him of murdering democracy in Kerala, Nehru said in the Lok Sabha, 'A story comes to my mind of an unfortunate young man who killed his father and mother. When he was hauled up before the court, he asked for clemency on the ground of being an orphan.' In one of the earliest speeches Nehru made soon after the 1962 Chinese invasion, he said,

> The Chinese invasion of India has begun a new phase in our nation's life. This is a turning point in our history. One chapter has ended and a new has begun. This is certainly a time of trial for each one of us. We should be firm in our resolve and we should steel our will to defend every inch of our territory. No nation can tolerate an attack on its dignity. We are an independent nation and we stand firm and erect in our independence. Each one of us will have to pay the price for preserving this independence. This challenge has come to us, perhaps, to pull us out of the soft and slow ways into which we had fallen. The first thing which we have to learn from this challenge is to put an end to all those tendencies which divide us. Internal dissensions or disputes, whether they are between one region and another or between one language and another have no place whatsoever in the circumstances of today. The national crisis demands that we should leave such things aside and think about the bigger and more important issues which face us. Therefore, I lay the greatest emphasis on the essential unity of India. We should work for the nation's progress and preserve its unity. Once the feeling of strength and unity is there, our task will be easy to accomplish.

Even though Nehru may have felt broken and cheated within him, he put up a brave fight before the nation and despite the war situation, his thinking and instincts remained firmly wedded to democratic norms. Underlining the spontaneous response of the people to the call of the nation in a time of crisis, Nehru felt that democracy was vindicated. He said, 'It should not be a case of losing our breath too soon. We may have to run long distances and we have to carry on with determination and fortitude for a long, long time.' Averse to sycophancy, Nehru once asked the Chairman of Rajya Sabha when a member stood up to speak on China and started praising Nehru, 'Mr. Chairman, would you kindly tell the Honourable Member that the subject under discussion is China, not me and my family.'

Following the severe reverses in the war with China suffered by India on account of the utter unpreparedness of the defence forces, there was a powerful uproar in the Parliament against Defence Minister Krishna Menon, an old-time close confidante and friend of Nehru. Despite his personal feelings, Nehru yielded to strong parliamentary pressure and asked

Menon to quit. Nehru also almost apologized to the House for having not kept it informed of the earlier Chinese incursions into Indian Territory. The Minister for Oil, Mines and Fuel, K.D. Malaviya also had to go as he was adjudged as being constructively responsible in some corruption charges. Nehru did not hesitate to institute inquiries in corruption cases even if it involved his favourite chief ministers, for example, Pratap Singh Kairon of Punjab and Biju Patnaik and Hare Krishna Mahato of Orissa. As early as in 1956–7, Nehru advocated some necessary parliamentary reforms including the setting up of departmental standing committees. Unfortunately, in the succeeding decades, till the 8th Lok Sabha, precious little was done in the setting up of departmental standing committees. I can take some personal pride, in all humility, for pursuing this matter and Nehru's reform suggestions in various forums in India and abroad almost single-handedly. I was a member of the Study of Parliament Group in Britain which recommended subject-based or department-related parliamentary committees to oversee administration, examine proposed legislations, and scrutinize budget proposals. Under the 1973 procedural reforms, such committees were established in the House of Commons. In India, however, we had to wait till 1989, when we finally succeeded in setting up three such committees. Incidentally, as the then Secretary General, I could say that I had something to do with conceiving and seeing the proposals through.

Participating in the debate on the Assam disturbances in the Lok Sabha on 3 September 1960, Nehru said, 'It is a very grave tragedy for people in one state to be driven out either by force or through sheer panic. Panic is so infectious that it is difficult to deal with it. It is terrible, this spectre of the old evil coming out. It is a symbol of our weaknesses, of narrowness of mind, of our incapacity.' It was to keep the nation wide awake to the bigger problems and to turn the peoples' minds to the guided path of national unity that a Conference on National Integration was held in Delhi in September 1961. Nehru said, 'It is bad to be narrow-minded ever, but it is worse to be narrow-minded when we are trying to change India.' Nehru has been criticized and may continue to be criticized for many things. For example, he has been criticized for accepting the Partition of India, for decimating by design the ideologically based healthy opposition and alternative to the Congress—the Praja Socialist Party, for having ditched Subhas Chandra Bose in Congress politics and for weakening the liberal

Left within the Congress by ousting the Socialists, for following an utopian China policy, for having referred the Kashmir issue to the UN perhaps under the influence of Mountbatten and for having agreed to plebiscite, and, finally, for his failure to bring about universal literacy in the country.

There will always be different assessments and viewpoint variants. But nothing can take away the memories of his disarming personal charm and the unique largeness of his heart. Nothing can change his place in history as the artificer of modern India and father of our parliamentary democracy. When Pandit Jawaharlal Nehru walked through the corridors of the Parliament House, the massive pillars got dwarfed. He won great respect and esteem on the world stage and, at one time, he became the conscience of the globe. Towards the later years of his life, Nehru was a man in a hurry. He saw the magnitude of the unfinished task, the miles to go, and the short time at his disposal. When the news of his demise came, it seemed that the earth shook. We rushed to Teen Murti Bhavan. I remember being a helpless member of a large equally helpless and sombre crowd for some hours. Jawaharlal Nehru, in life as in death, was treated as one of the noblest souls of the nation by his countrymen and by the world at large.

Amply realizing this collective sentiment of the nation much before his death, Nehru had inter alia said in his will,

> I have received so much love and affection from the Indian people that nothing I can do can repay even a small fraction of it. And indeed, there can be no repayment of so precious a thing as affection. Many have been admired, some have been revered, but the affection of all classes of the Indian people has come to me in such abundant measure that I have been overwhelmed by it.

Neither the history of Indian parliamentary democracy nor Jawaharlal Nehru's role in its evolution came to an end on 27 May 1964. Nehru lives on, his legacy lives on as India and her democratic polity grows from strength to strength. Nehru's ideas continue to inspire and guide the nation on its onward march to greatness.

MUCHKUND DUBEY

4

Nehru's Vision of the International Order

My acquaintance with Pandit Jawaharlal Nehru was almost nonexistent and my contacts with him were of an impersonal and fleeting nature. I recall seeing him from close quarters hoisting the national flag at the ramparts of the historic Red Fort where I was posted on duty as an Indian Foreign Service probationer. I would occasionally see him entering into and exiting out of the South block when I was receiving my training in the ministry.

I recall meeting him at his residence in the Teen Murti Bhavan when he called us for what was billed as our final interview in the Service but it turned out to be a pep talk by the prime minister of India to the young probationers of that batch. He dwelt on the tremendous changes that had been brought about by advances in science and advised us to be constantly alert and prepared to meet the challenges posed by these changes. Very few of his contemporaries were as acutely conscious of the changes taking place around them and as constantly engaged in sifting and evaluating them with a view to formulating and adjusting policies, as was Pandit Jawaharlal Nehru.

The First United Nations Conference on Trade and Development (UNCTAD), a momentous event in the annals of the United Nations, was in full swing in Geneva when Panditji died on 27 May 1964. I was the Member Secretary of the Indian delegation to the Conference. I happened to be the first to see the news of Panditji's demise and had the tragic duty of bringing it to the attention of the leader of the Indian delegation. When the President and the Secretary General of the Conference came to know about it, they arranged a Special Session of the Plenary, devoted to Jawaharlal Nehru. Most eloquent tributes, giving vent to the high esteem in which Nehru was held all over the world, started pouring in at that Session from all quarters. Even though it was not necessary, the Chairpersons of all the five Committees of the Conference in their response to that world-shaking tragedy, interrupted the proceedings of their Committees in order to pay tribute to Jawaharlal Nehru. Sitting through these sessions I was convinced that I was privileged to have worked under a Foreign Minister of India who was not only the tallest Indian leader but also one of the greatest leaders of the modern era.

I feel really proud to have devoted my entire career in the Indian Foreign Service to understand, interpret, and implement the foreign policy laid down by Jawaharlal Nehru. In our understanding of and approach to international issues, we were deeply influenced by his perceptions and philosophy. I, on my part, always followed his precept that though the furtherance of national interest is of paramount importance in the conduct of foreign policy, a principal task in the pursuit of multilateral diplomacy must be to advance the wider cause of the international community. In his speech in the United Nations General Assembly delivered on 20 December 1956, Panditji said: 'I hope that gradually each representative here, while obviously not forgetting the interests of his country, will begin to think that he is something more than the representative of his country that he represents in a small measure perhaps, the world community.' I was imperceptibly but decidedly guided by this philosophy throughout my diplomatic career, particularly during the process of formulating the International Development Strategies for the 1970s and 1980s, and while developing a global consensus on the different facets of the link between disarmament and development.

Nehru was one of the handful of leaders during his time who had a clear vision of the international order. Nehru's vision of the international order was different from those of other world leaders because it was shaped by his unique background, particularly by his experience of waging the struggle for India's independence under the stewardship of Mahatma Gandhi. In the conception and articulation of his vision of the international order, Nehru was profoundly influenced by Gandhiji's teachings. He imbibed the Gandhian ideals through his long intimate contact with the Mahatma. He was in the vantage position of seeing Gandhiji practising these ideals in his day-to-day life. Gradually, he became a firm believer of these ideals and practised them with modifications and adaptations. An American scholar, Willard Range, in the Introduction of his book *Jawaharlal Nehru's World View*, has summed up Gandhiji's influence on Nehru in the following words: 'His goal seems to be to adapt Gandhiji's teachings to international relations; and although it has required much modifying, cutting and refitting, the basic principles of the Gandhi philosophy are evident throughout.'

Nehru's vision of the international order converged in a system which Nehru thought should replace the then capitalist system lock, stock and barrel. Nehru saw the old capitalist system decaying and on the verge of collapse under the burden of its inherent weaknesses and contradictions. He had been witness to the unfolding of the worst possible forms and manifestations of capitalism. It had virtually collapsed during the great depression of 1929. Subsequently, it degenerated into Fascism in Italy and Nazism in Germany. Nehru was also witness to as well as the victim of its imperialistic and colonial manifestation. He had firsthand knowledge of its propensity to exploit, oppress, and brutalize the subject peoples, its record of suppressing freedom and extinguishing human rights, and its utter insensitivity to the basic urges of the masses.

Towards the end of the 1940s, Nehru asserted: '... present day civilization is ending and out of its ashes a new civilization will be built up'. He thought that the pre-War type of capitalism, particularly the type emphasizing the laissez-faire philosophy was already in the process of disintegration. It was 'a kind of a luxury system for well-to-do nations', he declared. The factors which spelt the inevitable doom of the capitalist system were the changes brought about by science and the demand of the masses for basic needs and security. He declared in 1940 that new forces such as elemental urges for freedom, food, and security were moving vast masses of people, and history was being moulded by the pressure of these forces. In 1951 and subsequently, he said that international relations were no longer the old game of chess, the old bargaining for territories and national wealth and resources among rulers. A whole battery of new factors had surfaced that made relations among states quite different from what they were before. There was, for example, a new weapons technology that threatened to unleash war on a hitherto unimagined scale and that rendered the whole international system of power politics out-of-date.

Nehru thought that internationalism was inevitable, whereas capitalism was fiercely nationalistic. He argued that by the later part of the nineteenth century, technological developments had so promoted the interdependence of States that an internationalized economy alone could serve the need of mankind properly. But the vested interests in the capitalist system opposed internationalism and clung to outworn economic nationalism, particularly high tariffs, monopoly practices, and cartelization.

In Nehru's view, competition, conflict, and exploitation were inherent characteristics of capitalism; and a system based on features wherein friction was inherent was not suitable in an interdependent world in which cooperation was essential. He said the capitalist system had shown no capacity to adjust to the new era being produced by science. It was high time, therefore, for capitalism to retire in favour of socialism, a system designed to promote international economic cooperation.

Nehru saw capitalism fighting a rearguard battle to preserve itself and the status quo. The disappointing thing about World War II to Nehru was that democracies showed no signs of fighting for a new order. Rather they were fighting for maintaining the old outworn system of the past.

Of course, Nehru had seen capitalism at its nadir. Since that time capitalist States have increasingly become democratic and have been trying to live down their unsavoury past of Nazism, Fascism, and Imperialism. Internally, they introduced heavy doses of socialism to convert themselves truly into welfare States. Externally, they took the initiative of putting in place a whole set of institutions for international cooperation, including the United Nations itself, the International Monetary Fund, the World Bank and General Agreement on Tariffs and Trade (GATT). They became the leaders in science and technology which in its latest phase has set in motion the process of globalization. But all this has happened within the framework of unequal relations between dominant and weaker countries and their asymmetrical positions in the international political and economic system. Leading capitalist countries are still resolved to preserve the status quo at all costs.

Nehru subsequently came to the conclusion that after all it was no longer necessary nor, indeed, feasible to uproot the capitalist system. All that was necessary was to continue to reform it through stronger and stronger injections of socialism until a new system combining both capitalism and socialism emerged.

Much before other leaders of his generation, Nehru had fully grasped the reality of economic interdependence among nations which subsequently figured very prominently in international discourse, particularly after the submission of the first Brandt Commission Report in 1980. It was Nehru who first advanced the oft-quoted idea that poverty anywhere is a danger to prosperity everywhere; he put it in his own words: 'Just as some infectious disease somewhere might be a danger to healthy conditions everywhere.' In his speech delivered in the Canadian Parliament on 20 October 1949, he said: 'Nor, indeed can there be a balanced economy for the world as a whole if the undeveloped parts continue to upset that balance and drag down even the more prosperous nations. Both for economic and political reasons, therefore, it has become essential to develop these undeveloped regions and to raise the standards of the people there.'

In the Asian Relations Conference in Delhi on 23 March 1947, he said: 'Economic interdependence, there is bound to be. No one can speak in terms of isolationism today.' He believed that the underdeveloped countries had the potential of becoming a better market for the products of the developed countries and a better source of supplies to them. Hence, assisting these countries was not a generosity on the part of the developed countries, but it was in their own enlightened self-interests.

Both Gandhi and Nehru had the vision of some form of a World Government. They called it by various names like 'one world', 'a united world' or 'a world union'. However, the term on which they focused most was 'a world federation' of independent and equal states.

Gandhiji said: 'My idea of nationalism is that, if need be, the whole of the country may die so that the human race may live ... Let that be our nationalism.' On another occasion he said: 'My nationalism is intense internationalism. I am sick of the strife between nations or religions.' In the Asian Relation Conference, when he was asked whether he subscribed to the theory of one world, Gandhiji said: 'I must confess to you that I would not like to live in this world if it was not to be one world. Certainly I would like to see that dream realized in my lifetime'.

As early as in the late 1920s, Jawaharlal Nehru told the Indian National Congress that once India was free he would favour a world federation even to having India give up part of her 'independence to a larger group of which she is an equal member'. Writing in the *National Herald* on 31 May/1 June 1939, Nehru said: 'A world union is necessary today ... It will not come before the world is shattered again by war and millions have perished. But it will come because there is no other way out.' In a Confidential Note written at Wardha on 25 August 1940, he said: 'This means the evolution of a new world order based on a different political and economic system which avoids conflict. This must lead to a world federation and the distribution of the world's resources fairly among different countries and peoples.' Interestingly, one of the most elaborate enunciations of the idea of world federation was in the Congress Resolution of 1942, which called upon the British to quit India. The relevant portion of the Resolution which was drafted jointly by Gandhiji and Jawaharlal Nehru, is worth quoting in extenso:

> While the All India Congress Committee must primarily be concerned with the independence and defence of India in this hour of danger, the Committee is of the opinion that the future peace, security and ordered progress of the world demand a world federation of free nations, as on no other basis can the problems of the modern world be solved. Such a world federation will ensure the freedom of its constituent nations, the prevention of exploitation by one nation over another, the protection of national minorities, the advancement of all backward areas and peoples and the pooling of the world's resources for the common good of all.

Thus the notion of one world for Nehru marked not merely a legal and institutional transition; it represented a total system transformation. It was a wholesale replacement of the existing order which he saw on the verge of collapse.

Until the end of the 1940s, Nehru was confident that the emergence of a world federation was inevitable. This was not only because of the inexorable march of science which dictated a complete re-ordering of international relations, not only because the old system was crumbling, but also because, as Nehru put it, 'millions yearned for it'. In a broadcast from New Delhi on 3 April 1948, Nehru said:

> I have no doubt in my mind that a world government must and will come, for there is no other remedy for the world's sickness. The machinery for it is not difficult to devise. It can be an extension of the federal principle, a growth of the idea underlying the United Nations, giving each national unit freedom to fashion its destiny according to its genius, but subject always to the basic covenant of a World Government.

However, with the passage of time, with the onset of the Cold War and the division of the world into two contending power blocs, with the galloping militarization of international relations, and with the commencement of and pace gathered by the nuclear arms race, Nehru realized the 'enormous difficulties' in realizing the idea of world federation. But even while the materialization of the idea became more and more distant, Nehru, until the end, refused to give it up or lose faith in its inevitability. In a speech in the Lok Sabha on 18 February 1958, he said, 'People talk about a united world; many wise, intelligent and ardent people advocate the ideal of world federalism'. As late in his life as October 1963, in his UN Day speech in New Delhi he said: 'In theory, I suppose many of us are stuck with the ideal of the whole world becoming an orderly world ... I suppose ultimately this is bound to happen unless the world destroys itself by war in the meantime.'

Gradually, Nehru came to believe that a lot of hard work would be required for realizing the idea of one world and that disarmament was a precondition for it. In his 1956 General Assembly speech, he said: 'One world can't just be brought into being overnight, it will emerge, emerge from the United Nations.' In one of his last major speeches on this issue, at the World Federalists' Conference in New Delhi on 5 September 1963, Nehru said: 'Disarmament is inevitably in it, otherwise there can be no world state. That is obvious. If you have disarmament, it seems to be inevitable that you should have some kind of World Authority and the world police force. All these raise enormous difficulties at the present moment. But these two are essential things.'

Nehru saw the United Nations as the closest possible approximation to his idea of one world. He, therefore, extended his full support to the United Nations in spite of its failures and fumbling. He was aware that the high hopes reposed in the United Nations had not been realized. But he firmly believed that the world will be much worse without this world organization and in any event if the United Nations disappeared, the international community will be obliged to create more or less a similar organization to replace it. In his message broadcast by the United Nations Radio network in New York, on 5 May 1950, Nehru said:

> It is true that the high hopes with which the United Nations Organization was started have not been fulfilled. At the same time, there can be no doubt that the mere fact of its existence has saved us from many dangers and conflicts. Also, there is no doubt that in the world of today, it is the only hope for finding a way for peaceful cooperation among nations. If the United Nations ceases to be or if it radically changes its position and nature, then there is nothing left which will inspire hope for the future ... The whole conception of One World, however distant that One World may be, involves an organization like the United Nations.

Regionalism is an indispensable tier of any international order. Nehru was aware of it and he tried to build the Asian tier of the World Order. That was one of the main purposes behind his convening the Asian Relations Conference in New Delhi in March 1947, even before India became independent. The Conference was a historic event in several respects, but Nehru did not succeed through this Conference, in giving an institutional shape to the Asian identity. There was no formal agreement even on the proposition of convening that Conference again. It was expected that the Chinese would take the lead in this regard, but nothing of this sort happened as the Chinese soon found themselves in the throes of a far-reaching revolution. The closing Plenary Session of the Conference decided to start an Asian Relations Organization with a Provisional General Council and Nehru was elected its President, but this decision remained on paper.

However, the Conference eminently served the purpose of giving a signal of the end of the old order and the beginning of a new order in the world. It gave an indication to the Western world which had dominated the world scene for the best part of the modern times, that other actors, from Asia and Africa, had emerged who were ready and insistent to play their due role in world affairs. Nehru announced at the Asian Relations Conference: 'Asia, after a long period of quiescence, has suddenly become important again in world affairs.' In his UN General Assembly speech in 1948, he warned: 'The World is something larger than Europe—the people in other parts are aware and moving.' And then came this soul-stirring pronouncement at the Asian Relations Conference: 'For too long, we of Asia have been petitioners in Western Courts and Chancelleries. That story must now belong to the past. We propose to stand on our own feet and to cooperate with all others who are prepared to cooperate with us. We do not intend to be the plaything of the others.'

Regionalism, according to Nehru, must be geared exclusively to peace, cooperation, and the establishment of a world order. He declared at the Asian Relations Conference: 'We have no designs against anybody; ours is a great design of promoting peace and progress all over the world.' He went further and said that 'Indeed, there can be no peace unless Asia plays her part' and that 'Asia must come together for one world'.

Nehru's conception of regionalism as a catalyst for world peace and security led him to oppose regional military pacts arrayed and aggressively competing against one another, and conceived in the context of hostility towards each other. According to Nehru, these were born out of fear, were predicated on reliance on military means, and had the effect of perpetuating hostility. Nehru here was referring to the North Atlantic Treaty Organization (NATO), Southeast Asia Treaty Organization (SEATO), Central Treaty Organization (CENTO) and the Warsaw Pact. He asserted that instead of solving the problems of the world, these associations might get in the way of desperately needed global cooperation.

The international order, according to Nehru, has to be an ideal order based on certain fundamental principles. An ideal order of Nehru's conception was not a Utopia by any chance. For Gandhi and Nehru, ideals were the very basis of conducting human relations. Gandhiji said in his article in *Harijan* on 5 September 1936, 'Non-Violence is the law of the human race and is infinitely greater than and superior to brute force.' For Nehru, cooperation was endowed with the same sanctity. It is cooperation which keeps the world going. Both Nehru and Gandhi demonstrated that these ideals can be practised to great effect and purpose in an individual's and national life.

The principles and ideals which Nehru wanted to be imported into his vision of the international order were those of Truth, Non-violence, Tolerance, Fearlessness, and the Common Good. Truth to the Mahatma was ultimately the quest for the divine through the chores of daily life. It was the search for divinity in humanity. To the agnostic mind of Nehru, truth could be approached through the process of reasoning or rationality, through an incessant search for the solution of the problems bedeviling human society, in a spirit of scientific enquiry and through the application of scientific method. In approaching truth in this fashion, Nehru was not borrowing from the West, but was firmly rooted in the Indian heritage. He was simply echoing what Buddha had once told his greatest disciple, Anand. 'Anand, do not believe in what the scriptures have said; do not believe in what the great sages of the past have said; do not believe even in what I have said; test everything on the touchstone of your knowledge and believe accordingly.'

In an international order based on truth, right must prevail over wrong; justice and fair play should prevail over tyranny and oppression; equality and distributive justice should prevail over irrational exploitative structures of colonialism and other forms of hegemony; and common good should prevail over blind pursuit of self-interests.

Non-violence as applied in international relations above all called for the demilitarization of these relations. That is why for Nehru, disarmament became the pre-condition for moving towards the goal of one world. Nehru was a strong critic of pacts and alliances, first and foremost, because they had the effect of perpetrating the cult of violence. They were based on the assumption of an enemy power or bloc and they led to the division of a region and the world into hostile camps. Because of their existence, a local war carried the danger of escalating into a world war. Nehru's belief in non-violence did not make him a pacifist or necessarily an advocate of unilateral disarmament. He believed in maintaining fully capable military forces to fight aggression.

What was important for him was the mental attitude that must be brought to bear on issues of defence and the attitude towards countries which are perceived as hostile. Nehru wanted totally to eschew hostility or fear in dealing with other countries irrespective of how hostile they themselves can become. He was against preparation for waging wars against other nations and he totally repudiated the Cold War against which he used some of the harshest words. In his speech at the Conference of All India Manufacturers' Organization, in New Delhi on 13 April 1957, he defined cold war as 'meaning all the apparatus of war and the hatred of war and the propaganda of war, without shooting, actual shooting and killing'. He then said that 'bad as the shooting and killing is, it is better than this continuous propagation of hatred which cuts into one's vitals' and prevents 'clear thinking or clear action'.

Tolerance for both Gandhi and Nehru was an absolute necessity for the kind of world order they were trying to promote. Nehru was enamoured by the rich diversity of the world and how it made living worthwhile. He believed that differences among people have always existed and will continue to exist. He thought that a pluralistic world society in which there is unending variety is much more interesting and exciting than a drab and regimented world based on intolerance. Nehru said that mankind will be better off with fewer crusades, with more tolerance, and with more of an attitude to live and let live.

Tolerance is essential for peace, as non-tolerance can lead to hostility culminating in military adventurism. That is why Nehru, along with other Asian leaders, pioneered the Panchsheel or the five principles of peaceful coexistence which is firmly anchored in the concept of tolerance. In the conduct of international relations, nothing expresses the ideal of tolerance more succinctly than the principle of peaceful coexistence. The spirit of tolerance breathes through the other four principles of Panchsheel also that is, (a) mutual respect for each other's territory, (b) non-aggression, (c) non-interference in each other's internal affairs, and (d) equality and mutual benefit.

Nehru was a firm believer in Gandhiji's tenet that fear is the worst enemy of mankind. It vitiates human relations as well as relations among nations. It is a major obstacle to overcome for building a structure of a new international order. In his various writings and speeches, Nehru repeatedly emphasized that fear clouded man's thinking and obstructed his reasoning faculty. It distorted values and brought about a decline in moral and intellectual standards. Above all, it promoted hatred and all that goes with it. It was fear which maintained the Cold War.

The Doctrine of Deterrence which Nehru described as 'the doctrine of peace by horror' and which has been mainly responsible for propelling the nuclear arms race, is essentially based on fear. Nehru said that the usual type of economic and political conflict was unlikely to precipitate anything so horrible as a third world war; but fear by one party of the increasing strength of the other might do so. In a broadcast from New Delhi on 3 April 1948, Nehru said: 'But fear is an ignoble emotion and leads to blind strife. Let us try to get rid of this fear and base our thought and actions on what is essentially right and moral ...'

Under the influence of Gandhiji who launched the biggest and the most successful mass movement ever witnessed in human history and through his own contacts with the masses of India, Nehru, like Gandhi, had made the betterment of the conditions of masses the touchstone of the success or failure of all his endeavours and exertions. He had taken to heart Gandhiji's vow of wiping every tear from every eye. Like Gandhi, the welfare of the masses was his talisman. Nehru believed that the ultimate objective of all systems—national as well as international—must be to promote the welfare of the common man. Thus, no international order would be worth its name if it did not accord primacy to human welfare or common good. Nehru once said that the degree to which a civilization has advanced could be measured by the degree of cooperation and sacrifice for the common good that the people of that civilization have learned to make.

To Gandhiji, man was essentially good. This could not be otherwise because he was a spark of the Divine. Gandhiji also believed that in the battle between the good and the evil, good is bound to prevail ultimately. Therefore, the primary task of social reformers and activists is to bring out the goodness in man and release his unbounded energy and creativity. To Nehru, man was neither good nor bad inherently. It was the system that made him good or bad. Therefore, the primary task of social and political leadership was to bring about a change in the old systems of feudalism, capitalism, and colonialism. Nehru believed that by the end of the 1940s, the old colonialism was on its last legs. In his address to the Asian Relations Conference he said: 'Today we have reached a stage when no country in Europe or elsewhere dares to base its prosperity on exploiting any other country.' However, Nehru was aware that though colonialism in the traditional sense was over; it was appearing in various new forms. That is why in his speech at the 1948 session of the UN General Assembly he promised 'an active struggle against any and every form of colonialism in any part of the world'.

Democracy was the essence of the new international order envisaged by Jawaharlal Nehru. In the international system, democracy found its concrete expression in the universality of international institutions. In a speech given by him in the Lok Sabha on 18 February 1953, Nehru said that 'the first attribute of the United Nations' was its universality. This is what, according to him, made the essential difference between the League of Nations and the United Nations. It is the concept of 'We the Peoples of the United Nations' enshrined in the UN Charter, which sets the UN apart from every other organization that was created before it. It was Nehru's uncompromising commitment to the principle of UN's universality which prompted India to take the initiative for the admission of the People's Republic of China to the United Nations—an initiative which India persisted with even after the Chinese committed an armed aggression against it.

To both Gandhiji and Nehru, the means adopted for bringing about a change in the old system and for establishing the new system were as important as the basic parameters and the objectives of the new system. Nehru was insistent that Gandhiji's teaching that means are always as important as ends must be applied also to the endeavour for establishing a new international order. In his 1948, UN General Assembly speech, Nehru said: 'the best of objectives may not be reached if our eyes are bloodshot and our minds clouded with passion'. He added that the lesson of history had been that 'out of hatred and violence only hatred and violence will come'. Nehru never missed any opportunity to emphasize this equivalence between the means and end. He returned to this theme in his UN General Assembly speeches in 1956 and 1960 also. In the 1960 speech, he said: 'I am equally concerned that if we aim at right ends, right means must be employed, good will not emerge out of evil methods. That was the lesson which our great leader Gandhi taught us, and though we in India have failed in many ways in following his advice, something of this message still clings to our minds and hearts.'

One of Nehru's objections to pacts and alliances was that they were based on a total mismatch between ends and means. While their avowed objective was to achieve peace and stability, the method they followed was one of hostility, militarization, and even aggression. In his 1956 General Assembly speech, Nehru said that if we desire peace then 'why should we not follow the path of peace? Why should we be led away by fears, apprehensions, hatreds and violence?'

Nehru was one of the relentless crusaders for disarmament in the world. Very few world leaders devoted as much time and energy to the task of disarmament as Nehru did. One of the most cogent and comprehensive enunciations of what should be independent India's disarmament policy is found in the Wardha Confidential Note of 25 August 1940. This Note contains most of the elements that should go into the making of total disarmament. And they are as valid today as they were in 1940.

Nehru writes in that Note that the Indian belief in the complete disarmament of all nation states derives from (a) its adherence to the principle of non-violence, and (b) from practical considerations arising from our understanding of world events. While conceding that no disarmament would be possible during the war, he insisted that even while the war was being carried on, the objective of full disarmament should be kept in view. He stated that even if one destroyed army, navy, aeroplanes, and chemical bombs, they would be reinvented as nobody can arrest the march of science. He, therefore, argued that for real disarmament, the causes of conflict and war must be abolished, and the causes, according to him, lay in political and economic structures in the world. This called for fundamental changes in political and economic structures and 'the evolution of a new world order based on a different political and economic system which avoids conflict'. This, according to him, 'must lead to a world federation and the distribution of world's resources fairly among different countries and people'. There are very few instances of the articulation of the case for complete disarmament as succinct, as lucid, as cogent, and as convincing as this note written by Nehru in 1940.

Subsequently, Nehru developed other arguments in favour of complete disarmament. In many of his speeches, he expressed his concern about the horrors of nuclear weapons. In his 1956 UN General Assembly speech he said: 'We can, however, lessen the chances of war and the fear of war, through disarmament.' In his 1960 UN General Assembly speech he said that 'the choice today in this nuclear age is utter annihilation and destruction of civilization or of some way to have peaceful coexistence among Nations'. He also said in that speech that time was running out and if no progress was made in the next three to four years only disaster awaited mankind. Thus, disarmament was necessary to prevent war and the consequent annihilation of mankind.

Nehru regarded the arms race as the biggest obstacle to the creation of 'one world'. This would materialize only after the achievement of total disarmament. The advent of nuclear weapons brought about a dramatic change in the situation. It transformed the concepts of war, defence, and aggression. It brought to the fore a whole new set of security doctrines, each more bizarre and horrifying than the preceding one. This included disabling first strike, mutually assured destruction (MAD), flexible response and discriminate deterrence. It was at the same time widely recognized that nuclear weapons were not weapons of war, but of mass annihilation. Even President Reagan admitted that 'a nuclear war cannot be won and must never be fought'.

Very few world leaders had grasped the ominouos implications of nuclear weapons as clearly and articulated them as forcefully as Gandhiji and Jawaharlal Nehru did. Writing in the *Harijan* in July 1946, Gandhiji referred to the 'supreme tragedy of the bomb'. He said, 'So for as I can see, the atomic bomb has deadened finest feelings that has sustained mankind for ages'. Replying to those who claimed that the atom bomb could be a stabilizing factor, Gandhiji said, 'Often does good come out of evil. But that is God's and not man's plans. Man knows that only evil can come out of evil, as good out of good.' In another article in the *Harijan* in September 1946, Gandhiji said, 'I regard the employment of the atom bomb for the wholesale destruction of man, women and children as the most diabolical use of science'. Describing his feelings after hearing the news of the wiping out of Hiroshima, Gandhiji said: 'Unless now the world adopts non-violence, it will spell certain suicide for mankind'.

In his 1960 UN General Assembly speech, Nehru called the nuclear age as the 'new age' and in his speech at the concluding session of the Anti-Nuclear Arms Convention on 18 June 1962, he described the nuclear bomb 'as an evil thing'. In his speech at the closing session of the Asian-

African Conference in Bandung on 22 April 1955, Nehru said that if there is another war, there will be total destruction of mankind. That is to say a third world war would bring us not only to the abyss of civilization and culture but would mean total destruction.

Nehru waged a relentless campaign against nuclear weapon testing. He was genuinely horrified by the far-reaching ominous implications of nuclear tests, particularly in the atmosphere and made it one of his life's missions to get it stopped. On 22 April 1954, he wrote an article in the *National Herald* under the title 'The Death Dealer', in reaction to the nuclear test conducted by the United States. It is an angry article written in a highly disturbed state of mind. The following paragraph from this article would show how agitated Nehru was at that time.

> Have words lost all their meaning and has man's mind lost all anchorage? For, this surely is the way to madness, and the great men who control our destinies are dangerous self-centred lunatics, who are so full of their conceit and pride of power that they will rather rain death and destruction all over the world than give up their petty opinions and think and act aright.

On the same day Nehru made a statement in the Lok Sabha in which he announced that among the steps to be taken now and forthwith, the Government of India was considering proposing: (a) some sort of a standstill agreement on nuclear testing, pending agreement on the discontinuance of production and stockpiling of weapons of mass destruction and (b) calling for an immediate private meeting of the sub-committee of the Disarmament Commission to consider the standstill proposal.

This was followed by a transmission to the Secretary General of the United Nations of a statement to the same effect, on 8 April 1954. After this, it was a story of incessant efforts by India in the UN forums to get nuclear testing stopped and banned, and the continuing prevarication of the nuclear weapon powers. Nehru continued through his speeches to bring a great deal of force and passion to the arguments for stopping nuclear explosions. In his speech at the concluding session of the Anti-nuclear Arms Convention held in Delhi in June 1962, Nehru said: 'I do not know how many hundreds of thousands children born and unborn are going to be affected. And that millions have already been affected. It seems amazing to me purely on grounds of decency that a thing like this could be continued.'

In no small measure due to the efforts mounted by India and like-minded countries, a Partial Test Ban Treaty (PTBT) banning atmospheric tests was signed in 1963. Mankind heaved a sigh of relief, even though France and subsequently China did not sign the Treaty. This must have brought tremendous personal satisfaction to Nehru. But by that time, conditions for nuclear disarmament had become more difficult and complex. Missiles had been developed and deployed; large stockpiles of nuclear weapons had been amassed; and various security doctrines had been developed to justify the nuclear arms race.

To sum up, Nehru had a clear vision of an international order which would replace the capitalist system which had been rendered outmoded by the changes brought about by science and was on the verge of collapse due to its inherent contradictions. Whereas the capitalist system was characterized by competition, conflict, and exploitation, the international order of Nehru's vision would be based on cooperation, inter-dependence, and distributive justice. The new international order would also be based on the fundamental principles of truth, non-violence, tolerance, fearlessness, and common good. Democracy, that is the universality of the institutions underpinning it, would be its essence. Nehru strongly believed in the notion of world government in the form of a federation of free nations. This would emerge from the United Nations. Developments in the post-Second World War period, particularly the onset of the Cold War and the nuclear arms race, led Nehru to tamper his belief in the inevitability of a new international order. He saw enormous difficulties in realizing the idea but never gave up his faith in it. He regarded disarmament as a pre-condition for creating a world government. He worked relentlessly till the end for achieving disarmament, particularly for arresting the nuclear arms race.

The world situation today is much less conducive to the realization of an international order of Nehru's vision than it was during his time. The United Nations which Nehru saw as an embryonic form of world government is enfeebled and changed beyond recognition. It has lost several of its Charter functions which have been transferred to the International Monetary Fund (IMF), World Bank, World Trade Organization (WTO) and, most recently, G-20. There has been deep erosion in the power and functions of nation-states. Though the notion of 'failed State' is yet to acquire international legal status, the principle of non-interference in the domestic affairs of states has been compromised by the UN's endorsement of 'right of protection'. Though the Cold War has ended, the international system continues to be dominated by major military and economic powers. The nuclear arms race has acquired ominous proportions. India itself has emerged as a de facto nuclear weapon power. Should we then dismiss Nehru's vision of the international order as utopian and unrealizable? Nehru himself would not have got reconciled to the status quo and confined himself to merely tinkering with it. He would have continued to strive for the realization of his vision of the world order with greater courage of conviction, firmer determination, and renewed vigour.

JAGMOHAN

5

Two Waves in the Ocean of Nehru's Life

Jawaharlal Nehru's life was an ocean of thoughts and deeds. There was hardly any aspect of public domain upon which he had not reflected and with which his programmes, policies, and actions were not linked. To deal with such a panorama in a short article is virtually impossible. I would, therefore, restrict myself to only two waves from the ocean of Nehru's life which had a special bearing on my work, first as a city planner and administrator and then as a Governor of Jammu and Kashmir.

Nehru and Cities

PERSONAL VISIT

As one who was concerned with the formulation and implementation of the Delhi Master Plan, I had the good fortune to come in contact with Nehru's thoughts on cities in general and Delhi in particular. In the middle of 1963, he very graciously visited my modest office in Vikas Bhavan, the first prefabricated structure put up in Delhi. This he did at the request of Bhagwan Sahya, Chief Commissioner, Delhi, whom he held in high esteem. Bhagwan Sahya was keen to show Nehru how office and fieldwork, connected with the implementation of the Master Plan, was being organized on scientific lines, how new principles and practices were being evolved for securing integrated urban development, and how financial self-sufficiency was being achieved by acquiring lands, with a small 'revolving fund', and leasing them out, on a rational and equitable basis, to meet the rising requirements for residential, industrial, commercial, institutional, and environmental purposes.

Despite his poor health, Nehru stayed in my office for about ten minutes, looked at various maps and charts, and asked me and Bhagwan Sahya a couple of searching questions,[1] particularly about the opposition of strong vested interests to the acquisition of all urbanizable lands. His visit, though brief, invigorated our sense of mission and prompted us to go ahead with the implementation of our development projects with greater courage and conviction.

As a matter of general interest and also as a part of my duty, I have studied a large number of books, reports, and plans about Delhi. But nowhere have I found a description of this city as captivating, insightful, and all-embracing as the one penned by Nehru in these words:

> Here we stand in Delhi city, symbol of India and the new. It is not the narrow lanes and houses of old Delhi or the wide spaces and rather pretentious buildings of New Delhi that count, but the spirit of this ancient city. For Delhi has been an epitome of India's history with its succession of glory and disaster, and with its great capacity to absorb many cultures and yet remain itself. It is a gem with many facets, some bright and some darkened by age, presenting the course of India's life and thought during the ages. Even the stones here whisper to our ears of the ages of long ago and the air we breathe is full of the dust and fragrance of the past as also of the fresh and piercing winds of the present. We face the good and bad of India in Delhi city which has been the grave of many empires and the nursery of a republic. What a tremendous story is here; the tradition of millennia of our history surrounds us at every step, and the procession of innumerable generations passes by before our eyes ...

It is easy to see how these few lines capture not only the soul of a great city and a great civilization but also the soul of a powerful mind which was imbued with a poetic passion and a profound sense of history. They have moved me as nothing else has done during my long date with Delhi. Thereafter, I have always looked at this rapidly expanding metropolis as a spiritual workshop of the nation, a cultural crucible for fashioning out new ideas and ideals which would harmonize its past, present, and future into a dynamic web.

INFLUENCE ON THE DELHI MASTER PLAN

I began to believe that the city is a living organism. Like a human entity, it should have both a structure and a soul. And a good master plan for the city would be one which would create a potent structure and a healthy soul. It would eliminate what was clumsy and cruel in the past and protect and preserve what was beautiful and benign. A holistic approach would constitute its inner core, and sustainable development would be its guiding star. Its ultimate aim would be to attain a higher quality of life and create a value-oriented city with a style and personality of its own.

With the above thoughts in mind, the Delhi Master Plan was finalized, and hundreds of 'integrated development projects' were executed. To give just one example of conservation and green development, about 2000 hectares of land around historical monuments was acquired, cleared of squatters and developed as city-forests, parts, and gardens. These included Hauz Khas (250 hectares), Tughlakabad (325 hectares) Jahanpanah (175 hectares), Chirag Delhi (75 hectares), Siri Fort (100 hectares), and so on. They now provide not only huge lungs to the city but also serve as a strong protective cover to its architectural and historical legacy. Nothing, I am sure, would have pleased Nehru more than these vast 'greens' which have brought 'fresh and piercing winds of the present' to the capital of the Republic.

A SPECIAL CORNER FOR SHAHJAHANABAD

There was a special corner in Nehru's heart for the old and historic city of Shahjahanabad. He wrote: 'It has a definite and positive atmosphere which you can feel when you go there, especially when you know something about its tremendous past. It tells you about the inner life of a nation, its cultural activities in many fields, its spiritual adventures and its voyages in the realm of thought and action.'

It was Nehru's romance with old Delhi that, in part, created an urge in me to write my first book[2] *Rebuilding Shahjahanabad—The Walled City of*

Delhi where I have brought out how this city has been a symbol of power and prestige in India; how it has been loved and nursed, coveted and desired, ravished and conquered, neglected and despised; and how all these imprints of history now stand woven in its physical and spiritual texture.

NEW IDEAS: CHANDIGARH AND BHUBANESHWAR

Though conscious of the importance of preserving healthy traditions, Nehru was, in the context of emergence of new ideas, aware of the need to sometimes adopt a new approach in toto. With regard to the Chandigarh project, in the implementation of which he took personal interest, he said: 'Let this be a new town, symbolic of the freedom of India, unfettered by the traditions of the past ... an expression of nation's faith in future.' He noted how powerfully Le Corbusier's ideas had affected Indian architecture and opened new avenues to it. In the same strain, he spoke about the new capital city of Orissa, Bhubaneshwar: 'The site is the ideal one. The past is represented by ancient temples, some of them famous for their artistry. Otherwise, there is a clean slate to write upon.'

LOVE FOR ARCHITECTURE

Nehru's love for architecture was rooted in its being an art of 'creative construction'. He often underlined: 'It is almost god-like to create; there cannot be a greater joy than it.' In 1940, he visited Srinagar. After seeing the miserable conditions prevailing there, his first reaction was: 'I wish that some great architect would take charge of the planning and rebuilding of Srinagar, that the river fronts should be attacked first of all, that slums and poor men's houses should be removed and airy dwellings and avenues take their place, and so much also done to convert it into a fairy city of dream-like beauty.'

SLUM ERADICATION

The existence of slums agonized Nehru. He wrote:

> Slums are a disease, which if not checked immediately, might well overshadow the beauty of our cities. I believe in no argument, economic or other, which is based on creation of slums, I have a horror of slums. I do not mind a person living in the open like a vagabond or a gypsy. I am a bit of vagabond myself and I like vagabonds and gypsies. I do not mind a person living in a mud-hut, I do mind

slums in cities; and I have often said if you cannot provide buildings for those living in slums, give them open space to live in and give them some social services like water supply, and sanitation. The rest will follow.

Nehru wanted high priority to be given to housing. He underlined: 'If human welfare is the objective, it is bound up with the house.' He advised the housing departments of the State and Central governments to provide two-room houses even to 'the lowest of the low income families'. It was because of Nehru's views on slums that the following provision was made in India's First Five-Year Plan:

> These slums are a disgrace to the country and it is a matter of regret that governments, both Central and State, have so far paid little attention to this acute problem. No city can be considered healthy which tolerates within itself the existence of a highly congested area. Slums are a national problem. From the national point of view, it is better to pay for the cost of clearing slums than to continue to pay the mounting cost of slums and suffer destructive effects upon human lives and property indefinitely.

SHADOWS BETWEEN VISION AND REALITY

Unfortunately, despite Nehru's refreshing views on city planning, slum eradication and housing for low-income groups, and a few valiant efforts[3] made here and there to translate his vision into a reality, the overall conditions in urban India have remained as miserable as before. There are two main reasons behind it. First, Nehru himself underestimated the tremendous magnitude and complexity of the problems embedded in ruthless social and economic forces at the national and international levels. Second, those entrusted with the task of tackling these problems showed no creative and constructive vision or will. They became prisoners of petty politics.

After Nehru was gone, with problems mounting at an accelerated pace, the living conditions in poorer areas of our cities started deteriorating sharply. Today, we have the dubious distinction of having the highest congestion rate in the world—about 19 per cent of the families in the city live in less than 10 square metres of space and about 44 per cent have only one-room accommodation. Most of our major cities have become a beehive of illegal constructions and encroachments. Mumbai is derisively called the Slum Capital of the world and Delhi nurses in its lap as many as 600 unauthorized colonies.

INSPIRATION FROM NEHRU'S BASIC IDEAS

If even now we draw inspiration from the basic ideas of Nehru about our cities, adopt a new implementational strategy and muster a strong and selfless national will, the current position, hopeless as it may seem, could still be retrieved. Our blueprint for the future must involve a new urban land policy which provides social justice and treats land as a resource to be used for the benefit of the poor migrants; a new approach towards shelter which recognizes that we have problems not of housing in the conventional sense, but of having a roof over the head; a new framework of urban institutions which answers the current and emerging requirements of growing metropolises; a new cadre of urban administrators who have the training and motivation to meet the new challenges; a new human settlement technology which helps in the growth of happy and harmonious communities; a new plan for 'outflanking' the industrial revolution, developing 'green and clean' technologies and evolving an integrated system of regional development in which villages, small and medium-sized towns, and metropolises are linked with one another like threads of a web.

'Show me your cities; and I will tell you about the cultural aims of your people.' So goes the saying. Surely, we are capable of higher cultural aspirations than our cities at present show. What we, perhaps, badly need today is a great architect not only for reorganizing our physical spaces but also for providing new contours to our mind.

Nehru and Kashmir

When I landed in the state of Jammu and Kashmir as Governor on 26 April 1984, I was driven straight to the Srinagar Raj Bhavan. On arrival, I was shown around the complex which, though small in comparison to other Raj Bhavans in the country, commanded a grand view of the Dal Lake, Shankaracharya Hill and Hari Parbat. My attention was especially attracted to an elegant 'verandah', overlooking the lush green lawns which seemed to be merging into the shimmering waters of the lake. I was told that whenever Jawaharlal Nehru came to Srinagar, he stayed in this building[4] and made it a point to sit in the 'verandah' and watch the gorgeous sunset over the hills and the lake. Later on, I myself experienced the bewitching glory of this sunset and imagined how much Nehru, who had a great eye for the beauty of nature, would have enjoyed it. I often recalled his poetic description of Kashmir, given in these inimitable words:

> Like some supremely beautiful woman, whose beauty is almost impersonal and above human desire, such was Kashmir in all its feminine beauty of river and valley and lake and graceful trees. And then another aspect of this magic beauty would come to view, a masculine one, of hard mountains and precipices, and snow-capped peaks and glaciers, and cruel and fierce torrents rushing down to the valley below. It had a hundred faces and innumerable aspects, ever-changing, sometimes smiling, sometimes sad and full of sorrow. The mist would creep up from the Dal Lake and, like a transparent veil, give glimpses of what was behind. The clouds would throw out their arms to embrace a mountain-top, or creep down stealthily like children at play. I watched this ever-changing spectacle, and sometimes the sheer loveliness of it was overpowering.[5]

My arrival at Kashmir, however, was not the time to watch its beauty but to deal with its deeply disturbed landscape. The state was in turmoil. For quite some time, trouble had been brewing. In mid-1983, an ugly anti-Indian demonstration, instigated by pro-Pakistani elements, had been allowed to be staged at the venue of the India-West Indies cricket matches. A senior Indian diplomat, Ravinder Mhatre, had been murdered by Kashmiri militants in the UK and Maqbool Butt, convicted for killing police officials, was hanged in Tihar Jail, Delhi. Practically, there was some agitation or the other every day. Terrorism in Punjab was at its peak; its infection was seeping into the Valley.

For tackling the raging storm, one of the measures that seemed necessary was to look into its epicentre and study in depth the fall-outs of various important decisions, taken from time to time, by the national and state leaders. Even otherwise, I believe in what Winston Churchill once said: 'The further backward you look the further forward you can see.'

What follows in the subsequent paragraphs of this section is the outcome of this study, so far as it relates to the role which Nehru played in dealing with the internal as well as external aspects of the Kashmir issue.

INTERNAL ASPECTS OF THE KASHMIR ISSUE

At the time of the Indian Independence the political stage of Kashmir was crowded with a variety of actors. There was the National Conference, headed by Sheikh Mohammad Abdullah. It dominated the Valley but had a limited influence in Jammu and Ladakh. It had developed a close rapport with the leaders of the Indian National Congress, particularly Jawaharlal Nehru, but its equation with the Muslim League was marked by hostility. Mirwaiz Moulvi Yusaf Shah, who had a wild and fanatical following in the downtown area of Srinagar city, was antagonistic both to the National Conference and to the Congress. Then, there was the Muslim Conference which had little following in the Valley but had acquired rapid strength amongst the Muslims of the Jammu region on account of its ideological affinity with the Muslim League. The Maharaja was yet another force. The Dogra Rajputs of Jammu considered him their own kith and kin. The relations between him on the one hand and Sheikh Abdullah and Pandit Nehru on the other were marked by mutual distrust and dislike.

All these actors were soon to play their part in the first act of the tragic Kashmir drama. The Maharaja was indecisive. Jinnah was impatient. Pandit Nehru was caught in between his idealism and the stark realities of the situation. Sheikh Abdullah, with streaks of megalomania and duplicity embedded deep in his mind, was nursing secret ambitions to carve out a virtual Sheikhdom for himself and his coterie. The Muslim Conference and Yusaf Shah were in touch with Jinnah's agents. Each one of these actors was pushed on the stage with illusions of his own and believed that the drama would end the way he desired. Consequently, there was confusion and inconsistency on the stage. Mistake after mistake was made. And Kashmir soon found itself in the whirlpool of national and international controversy and conflict.

The first grave mistake was made when Maharaja Hari Singh flirted with the idea of independence. Jinnah's overconfidence led him to engineer a tribal invasion of Kashmir in the third week of October 1947. When the raiders were virtually on the doorsteps of Srinagar, the Maharaja asked for help and offered accession of the state to India. This help was superbly organized. The heroic acts of the armed forces saved the state by a whisker. But the triumph was marred by a political blunder. While accepting accession, Lord Mountbatten needlessly added: 'It is my Government's wish that, as soon as law and order have been restored in Kashmir and her soil cleared of the invaders, the question of the State's accession should be settled by a reference to the people.' This blunder was compounded by the inclusion of 'Plebiscite under the UN auspices', in Nehru's radio broadcast on 28 October.

On 1 January 1948, India took the case to the Security Council under Part VI, and not VII, of the United Nations Charter. This was another serious mistake. The decision to agree to 'cease-fire', when India was in position to push back all the raiders beyond the border, added to the list of grievous errors of judgement which Nehru made at the initial stages of handling the Kashmir issue. But his biggest failure was to judge the mind and motivation of Sheikh Abdullah. Jawaharlal Nehru placed too great a reliance upon him, but he proved a fair-weather friend. The moment Nehru declared that plebiscite would be held in the state; Sheikh Abdullah calculated that India could not do without his support. He exploited the position to extract one concession after another.

For Sheikh Abdullah, it was his power game that got precedence over everything else. What suited him at a particular moment was all that mattered. When it suited him, he kept proclaiming that accession of Kashmir to India was based on fundamental principles and was irrevocable. At the same time, he was sounding various quarters for support to the idea of having an independent 'Sheikhdom'. As early as 28 January 1948, he discussed the subject of independence with American officials. This is evident from the note of the same date sent by Warren Austin to the State Department after an interview with Sheikh Abdullah. The report (September 1950) of Loy Henderson, the US Ambassador to India, noted: 'In discussing future-Kashmir, Abdullah was vigorous that it should be independent'. On 3 May 1953, Adlai Stevenson came to Srinagar and had a long meeting with Sheikh Abdullah. The *New York Times*, in its issue of 5 July, published a map hinting at independent status for the Valley. On 10 July, speaking at Mujahid Manzil, Abdullah said, 'A time will, therefore, come when I will bid goodbye to India.'

All these events and pronouncements, taken together, should leave nobody in doubt that Sheikh Abdullah was dreaming of becoming an independent ruler of Kashmir and the Anglo-US bloc was encouraging him. Clement Attlee even openly said: 'Kashmir should belong to neither India nor Pakistan but should be independent.'

Even with regard to the Delhi Agreement (1952), for which Nehru was severely criticized in Parliament and other public fora, the stance of Sheikh Abdullah proved insincere. After securing implementation of what suited him, he virtually backed out. Nehru was deeply dismayed by his crafty approach. On 28 June 1953, he wrote to Abdullah: 'To me, it has been a major surprise that settlement arrived at between us should be repudiated. That strikes at the root of all confidence. My honour is bound with my words.' But Abdullah was unmoved.

It was Sheikh Abdullah's excessive ambition, rank opportunism, and virtual conspiracy to carve out an independent state that led to his arrest in August 1953. After Sheikh's arrest, both Bakshi Ghulam Mohammad and G.M. Sadiq adopted a constructive attitude and helped in establishing a working constitutional relationship between the state and the Union. However, Article 370 of the Indian Constitution, with elements of separatism inbuilt in it, remained.

Apart from a short period of release in 1958, Sheikh Abdullah was freed in April 1964 and, on the insistence of Nehru, the Kashmir Conspiracy case against him was withdrawn by the state government. In the wake of the revival of friendship between Sheikh and Nehru, the former visited Pakistan and had a meeting with President Ayub Khan on 25 May. President Ayub Khan, in his book, *Friends and Not Masters*, has recorded: 'When Sheikh Abdullah and Mirza Afzal Beg came to Pakistan in 1964, they had brought the absurd proposal of a confederation between India, Pakistan, and Kashmir. I told them plainly we should have nothing to do with it.' Nehru's death on 27 May caused Abdullah to return to Delhi.

Soon thereafter, Sheikh Abdullah reverted to his old game. In February 1965, he went abroad with his wife ostensibly for the purpose of Haj. But during this visit, he indulged in political propaganda which was highly embarrassing to India. On 28 March 1965, he even met Chou En Lai, Prime Minister of China. This meeting was seen as Abdullah's willingness to become a tool in the 'Pindi-Peking conspiracy' against India in respect to Kashmir. His passport was, therefore, cancelled. On return, he was arrested at Delhi Airport on 9 May 1965.

Nehru has to share a major portion of the blame for misjudging Sheikh Abdullah, the core of whose personality comes out clearly in his observations on Nehru in his autobiography, *Atish-e-Chinar*:

Nehru used to call himself an agnostic. But he was also a great admirer of the past heritage and the Hindu spirit of India ... His interpretation of the Indian history, though not always based upon accurate knowledge, approximates to the interpretation of revivalists like K.M. Munshi and Dayanand Saraswati ... Nehru employed Machiavellian approach towards us in Kashmir. He dealt with Pakistan in the same fashion. At international level also he exhibited the same Machiavellian outlook.

Nehru misjudged his political foes as well as his 'friends'. The real culprit was the politics of deception and duplicity initiated by Sheikh Abdullah. Had he shown even a modicum of sincerity with regard to the issue of accession, most of the subsequent troubles and turmoil could have been avoided.

EXTERNAL ASPECTS

While Nehru's handling of the Kashmir issue at the domestic level was marred by various errors of judgement and other infirmities, the story of his stand on international level is quite different. He refused to be browbeaten by the strongest of the power-blocs at the United Nations Security Council. Unfortunately, an impression persists in a sizeable section of the Indian public that even with regard to the international aspects of the Kashmir issue, the matter was inadequately dealt with by Nehru. This impression, as would be seen from what follows, is not at all well-based.

India's mistake in taking the Kashmir issue to the Security Council of the United Nations and that, too, under Chapter VI, and not Chapter VII[6] of the United Nations Charter, has already been noted. The gravity of the mistake looked all the more ominous when, at the very inception of the proceedings, India encountered hostile environment, engineered largely by the back-door machination of the UK delegate.[7] Her simple plea that Pakistan, which had organized the invasion, should be asked to vacate its aggression was deftly sidetracked and it was resolved that 'the problem had to be considered as a whole and the cessation of hostilities could not be treated apart from the prospect of the final settlement of the dispute'.

Nehru was outraged. He took a firm stand against the politics of power and intrigue. He did not even hesitate to express his indignation bluntly over India and Pakistan being treated on equal footing. Once when Josef Korbel, an influential member of the United Nations Commission for India and Pakistan, asked Nehru whether he would consider an unconditional cease-fire order, he shot back: 'It is your duty, as a Commission, to condemn

Pakistan for having an army on our soil. Otherwise, it would be as though a thief had broken into my house and you would treat the thief and the owner of the house as equals. First, the thief must get out.'

As a historical backdrop, I may indicate that the United Nations Commission for India and Pakistan, which had earlier been set up by the Security Council in accordance with its Resolution of April 1948, adopted, on 13 August 1948, a Resolution which laid down the basis for all its future action as well as of the subsequent deliberations at the Security Council.

The Resolution of 13 August 1948 is of pivotal importance. It has three parts. Part I pertains to the 'cease-fire'. Part II stipulates that Pakistan would withdraw its troops,[8] that all tribesmen and Pakistan nationals would be made to leave, and that, thereafter, India would begin to withdraw bulk of its forces. The requirement of Part III is that both India and Pakistan 'would reaffirm the principle that the future of the state shall be determined in accordance with the will of the people'. Both the parties, after holding separate discussions with the representatives of the Commission, accepted the Resolution and declared cease-fire which became effective from 1 January 1949.

Here too, Nehru showed no weakness. Before agreeing to the Resolution and cease-fire, India had, during the course of discussions with the Commission, obtained as many as eight assurances, including those that specified that 'the responsibility for the security of the state of Jammu and Kashmir would rest with the Government of India', that there 'shall not be any recognition of the so-called Azad Kashmir government', and that the plebiscite proposal shall not be binding upon India if Pakistan does not implement Part I and Part II of the Resolution.

Nehru left no one in doubt about what he thought of those who, out of bias or other considerations, were inclined to see holes in India's stand on Kashmir. When Loy Henderson,[9] Ambassador of the United States, commented that India seemed to be deviating from its pledge to hold plebiscite in Kashmir, Nehru, casting aside diplomatic veneer, replied:

I am tired of receiving moralistic advice from the United States. India did not need advice from any other country as to its foreign and internal policies. Our record is one of honesty and integrity, which did not warrant admonitions. So far as Kashmir is concerned, I would not give an inch. I would hold my ground even if Kashmir, India, and the whole world go to pieces.

Nehru also repelled various suggestions emanating from President Truman,[10] President Dwight Eisenhower and Prime Minister Attlee. He made no secret of his disappointment over what he considered was an 'equivocal attitude' of the United States and United Kingdom. And when, in 1954, Pakistan joined the Western Treaty Alliances and obtained American military aid, Nehru responded by declaring that 'the military pacts had destroyed the roots and foundations of the plebiscite proposal in Kashmir'. He also demanded the withdrawal of eighteen American military observers, as 'they could no longer be treated as neutrals in the dispute'.

Nehru handled the seemingly adverse development regarding Treaty Alliances in such a subtle manner that the tide was turned in favour of India. The USSR abandoned its earlier stance of neutrality and started supporting India at the Security Council. It did not hesitate to even use its veto power, whenever any resolution, hostile to the interest of India, was introduced in the Council.

During the visit of Nikolai Bulganin and Nikita Khrushchev to India in 1955, they went to Kashmir, where the latter declared: 'The future of Kashmir should be decided by the people themselves, and they have already decided to join India.' All this considerably strengthened India's hand in dealing with the Kashmir issue at international fora.

Soon after the Chinese aggression of 1962 against India, both the United States and Great Britain offered military assistance to it. Both calculated that India's discomfiture had left Nehru with little manoeuvrability on Kashmir, and it was a good time to obtain some concessions from him, settle the 'dispute' and prepare both India and Pakistan to counter the rising power of communist China in South Asia and South East Asia. President Kennedy sent a high-level political and military mission, headed by W. Averell Harriman, Assistant Secretary of State for Far Eastern Affairs, to New Delhi. He hoped that, 'with nursing from us', a settlement could be reached between India and Pakistan. A similar mission with similar objectives was sent by Great Britain. It was headed by Duncan Sanday, Secretary of State for Commonwealth Relations.

Even when India faced critical conditions, both Harriman and Sanday failed to secure any basic change in Nehru's stand. He made it clear that he was not prepared to go beyond a few minor adjustments in the 'cease-fire line'. After six rounds of talks had been held between the representatives of India and Pakistan, with US and British diplomats staying in the 'ante chamber', Nehru declared in August 1963: 'There is no question of considering any proposal for internationalization or division of the valley or joint control of Kashmir and the like.'

Nehru's handling of the external aspects of the Kashmir problem was marked by subtle deftness and firmness. Neither the mighty Western bloc nor the mighty Presidents of the United States could cut much ice with him. President Kennedy later told senior officers of the State Department that it was difficult to obtain any concession from Nehru on Kashmir as it was a 'bone-deep issue' with him.

MIND AND SOUL RELATIONSHIP

Whether Nehru was dealing with internal or external aspects, Kashmir's 'overpowering loveliness', about which he spoke in his description quoted earlier, and its centuries-old links with the mainland remained a part of Nehru's intellectual sub-consciousness. Unfortunately, most people in the world look at the Kashmir problem from communal and legal angles only. Hardly anyone realizes that India has never accepted the two-nation theory and that Kashmir's relationship with the rest of India is based not merely on the Instrument of Accession and Articles 1 and 370 of the Constitution of India; it is rooted in far more potent and enduring forces which neither the turbulence and tornadoes of the past nor the negativism and nihilism of the present-day politics can really destroy. It is a relationship of the mind and soul that has existed from time immemorial and has found ample expression in common avenues of intellect and emotions, poetry and literature, philosophy and outlook. Every green pasture that one walks around in Kashmir, every silvery peak that one watches from pleasurable distances, every stream that sings its song, every enchanting lake that one comes across now and then, and every little town and city that one visits, has some signpost of this deep and abiding relationship.

Notes

1. Interestingly, one question pertained to the relationship of the Delhi Development Authority with the Delhi Municipal Corporation. Presumably, as a Chairman of the Allahabad Municipal Board (1923–25) he had in view his own experience of dealing with the Allahabad Improvement Trust. This, incidentally, is what he wrote about his work in the Board: 'What I feared and disliked I have

begun to like, and municipal work has begun to have some fascination for me. I feel that it is in the power of our board to make life a little more bearable, a little less painful to the inhabitants of Allahabad.'

2. This book contained quite a few observations of Nehru. His wife, Kamla, came from a family who lived in Bazar Sita Ram, the heart of Shahjahanabad. Incidentally, the book brought me a cultural award from the Australian Government.

3. These efforts include the successful completion of the Capital-projects of Chandigarh, Bhubaneshwar, and Gandhinagar; Laurie Baker's 'Home-grown buildings' in Kerala; massive construction of Janta, low-income and middle income housing in Delhi; and resettlement of about 0.7 million slum-dwellers in 41 newly developed resettlement colonies in the same city.

4. At that time, the building was being used as government guest house. Later on, it became Governor's residence.

5. Nehru, Jawaharlal, *The Unity of India*. This description was recorded by Nehru in 1940.

6. While Chapter VII of the Charter deals with acts of aggression, chapter VI (Articles 34 & 35) merely enables the Security Council to recommend 'appropriate procedures and methods of adjustment for the pacific settlement of dispute'.

7. The attitude of Philip Noel Baker, Secretary of State for Commonwealth Relations in the Attlee government, and Lord Ismay, his adviser, was throughout anti-India. They also attempted to influence the views of the government of the United States, and often succeeded in bringing them in line with their thinking. However, at one stage, the American delegate had made it clear to the delegates of the UK that it was difficult to deny the legal validity of Kashmir's accession to India.

8. It may be noted that in the Commission's requirement that Pakistan should first withdraw its troops was an implicit acceptance by the United Nations of India's accusation that Pakistan had violated international law and committed aggression.

9. Loy Henderson was a bitter opponent of Nehru's foreign policy of Non-alignment. He seized every opportunity to needle India. The conversation between Nehru and Henderson, quoted here, took place in August 1949.

10. President Truman supported the proposal of the United Nations Commission for India and Pakistan regarding arbitration by Admiral Nimitz. He wrote to the prime ministers of both India and Pakistan. While Liaqat Ali accepted the President's suggestion, Nehru rejected it. Later, neither the McNaugton plan for demilitarization nor the Sir Owin Dixon formula for a limited plebiscite nor Dr Graham' proposals of mediation could make Nehru change his stand. Likewise, President Eisenhower' suggestions, based largely on the Dixon formula, were not agreed to, though he was given a tumultuous welcome when he visited India in 1959 and received what Nehru called a priceless gift—a part of India's heart.

BALRAJ PURI

6

Nehru's Kashmir Policy

Jawaharlal Nehru was well informed about Kashmir. He mentions it in *Glimpses of World History* in which he quotes *Rajatarangini* written by the celebrated historian Kalhana to describe the glory of ancient Kashmir. He comes to the formation of the present state when British East India Company sold Kashmir to Raja Gulab Singh of Jammu for Rs 70 lakh under the Treaty of Amritsar in 1846.[1] He described his visit to Kashmir in 1940, in a series of five articles in the *National Herald* as a passionate lover of a bewitching damsel personified by Kashmir.

Nehru was well aware of the sentiments of the Kashmiris who regarded the rule of Gulab Singh and his successors as an alien rule and who, though overwhelmingly Muslim, were conscious of their Kashmiri identity. As the Indian National Congress stood for responsible democratic governments in all princely states, Nehru had no hesitation in supporting the Kashmiri urge for the same. The Indian Muslim League, on the other hand, was patronized by the Nawabs and feudal lords. Hence it could not support the anti-Maharaja movement in Kashmir.

Nehru was indeed a major influence in converting the Muslim Conference, formed in 1931, into the National Conference in 1939. The support of the major national party for their demand was a big gain for the people of Kashmir. Nehru's Kashmiri origin added to his popularity in Kashmir. During his visit to Kashmir on 1 August 1945 along with other senior Congress leaders, where he got a royal reception organized by the National Conference, he said in his address, 'I am proud to be a Kashmiri; Kashmiriyat is in my blood and in my heart and mind.'[2]

The Kashmir movement gradually acquired greater militancy, partly under the influence of the communists who at that time were championing the cause of regional movements throughout the country. By May 1946, Sheikh Abdullah launched the Quit Kashmir movement which demanded abrogation of monarchy.

But some elements in the Congress had reservations about the call of the Sheikh as the party merely demanded responsible governments under the rulers of the princely states. But Nehru was quick to neutralize it. He rushed to Kashmir to lend support to it and donned the robes of a lawyer after ages, to plead the case of Abdullah in the court which was trying him on the charge of sedition. As a via media between the official stand of the Congress and the Quit Kashmir movement, he said that the movement was addressed not to the person of the Maharaja but to the institution of absolute monarchy and that though it exceeded the stand of the Congress, it did not contradict it. Later he deputed Asaf Ali and Dewan Chaman Lal to be Sheikh's defence lawyers.

A year later when the interim government with Nehru as head was about to be formed, he again travelled to Kashmir in June 1946. But he was stopped at the border of the state and asked by the state administration to return. On his refusal to do so, he was arrested and put up in a state guest house at Uri. As per his press statement, he refused to return till he got freedom to move throughout Kashmir.[3] Thereupon, Maulana Azad, who was then president of the Congress, 'ordered' Nehru to return as a disciplined soldier of the party.

Nehru did return but insisted that he would go to Kashmir again at the first available opportunity as Abdullah was his most precious friend and that in his hour of trial, he and his colleagues were with the people of Kashmir.[4] The Maharaja refused to show any leniency on his entry into the state. A compromise was reached according to which Mahatma Gandhi, instead, would go to Kashmir to which neither Nehru nor the Maharaja had any objection.

Gandhi also undertook not to address any public meetings except to hold prayer meetings which were organized by the National Conference and were well attended. He, however, made two brief statements. At the border he told press reporters that after the lapse of British sovereignty over the princely states, it has reverted to their people who alone were entitled to decide their future. In his second statement he said that in the benighted subcontinent he found a ray of light only in Kashmir.[5]

Gandhi reached Srinagar on 1 August 1947, when there was communal massacre in the two new dominions that were getting independence. The two statements of Gandhi had an electrifying impact on the Kashmiri people who still quote with pride the certificate of the Father of the Nation for maintaining complete communal harmony amidst bloodshed all around.

Nehru was not only deeply involved in the politics of Kashmir, more than any other national leader, he also encouraged an active role of Sheikh Abdullah in national politics. Nehru was elected President of the All India States People's Conference (AISPC) in December 1945 with Sheikh Abdullah as its Vice President. He would have been the acting President when Nehru joined the interim government in 1946, but it did not happen as he was in prison at that time.

At the time of fresh elections to the AISPC, Nehru said that 'the right choice for the presidentship is Sheikh Abdullah for he has become the symbol of freedom movement not only for the people of Kashmir but also for the people of other states.' He persuaded all other candidates for the post, including Jayaprakash Narayan (JP), to withdraw their names. Dwarkanath Kachru, secretary to Nehru, in his letter to JP, dated 7 March 1947, wrote 'Your name has been proposed for presidentship of the AISPC. You will, of course, withdraw in favour of Sheikh Abdullah ... It would be an expression of our solidarity and unity of interest with the people of Kashmir, if we elect Sheikh Abdullah president of the Conference.'[6] JP did accordingly and the Sheikh was elected unanimously while still in jail.

Another major development that brought Nehru and Abdullah closer to each other was Governor General Lord Mountbatten's announcement on 3 June 1947 of the plan for the partition of India into two dominions of India and Pakistan. Muslim League leader Mohammad Ali Jinnah unequivocally declared that constitutionally and legally the princes as independent and sovereign would be free to adopt any course they liked. He said that if they (rulers) wanted they could remain independent.[7] Nehru and the Congress did not admit the right of any ruler to take a decision against the wishes of the people.[8] Gandhi affirmed in one of his prayer meetings in Delhi that the real rulers of all the states were their people. The people of Kashmir, he said, 'without any coercion or show of force from within or without, must by themselves decide the issue'.[9]

This was in consonance with the stand of the National Conference which had stated that sovereignty belonged to the people. Thus while Nehru and the government headed by him earned a lot of goodwill in Kashmir, in Jammu the reaction was adverse. The Maharaja was apprehensive that Nehru might be vindictive for the way he was treated in the state. Moreover, he did not want to forego his right to decide the future of the state.

Jammu Leaders Support Independence

The Muslim Conference and Hindu Sabha, which were mainly based in Jammu, expressed loyalty to the Maharaja. Chaudhary Hameed Ullah, a leader of the former in a press statement at Jammu on 10 May 1947 urged His Highness to declare Kashmir independent immediately. He offered the cooperation of Muslims to carry out this policy and 'to welcome the Maharaja Bahadur as the first constitutional ruler of independent and democratic state'. The Muslim Conference of Jammu had opposed the Quit Kashmir Movement launched by Sheikh Abdullah in Kashmir 'as the Maharaja belonged to Jammu and its people were loyal to him'. The rift between the Jammu and Kashmir units of the Muslim Conference, the latter led by Mirwaiz Yusuf, became open. The Jammu Muslim Conference got recognition from the President of the Indian Muslim League while Mirwaiz disowned the League as well.[10]

The Hindu Sabha had an additional reason to be loyal to a Hindu Maharaja. A soft corner for him had by now developed in the right-wing parties in the rest of India also. The Rashtriya Swayamsevak Sangh (RSS) Chief, Guru Golwalkar visited Jammu as his personal guest. A letter from Sardar Patel to Jinnah has been widely quoted by many Pakistani commentators in which Patel offered Kashmir to Pakistan in exchange of

Hyderabad. I have not been able to get a copy of the original letter though some friends have confirmed it.

Campbell-Johnson attests to the fact that the State Ministry under Patel's direction went out of its way to take no action which could be interpreted as forcing Kashmir's hand and to give assurance that accession to Pakistan would not be taken amiss by India.[11]

The Maharaja's Prime Minister Ram Chand Kak visited Pakistan and met its Prime Minister Liaquat Ali Khan. What transpired between them was not made public.

Jinnah's personal secretary Khurshid Ahmed who stayed in Kashmir during those eventful days for several months, assured His Highness that 'Pakistan would not touch a hair of his head or take away an iota of his power' if he opted for accession to that country.[12]

Nehru cultivated friendship with Abdullah without insisting on a public commitment from him on the issue of accession. Though the latter was basically a leader of Kashmiri nationalism, Nehru was sympathetic to its aspirations. He was, therefore, confident that their common basic ideology and emotional attachment would enable him to accommodate Kashmiri nationalism within Indian nationalism. Pakistan, on the other hand, was banking on the Maharaja's distrust of Nehru and Abdullah and tried to reach an understanding with him either for the state's accession to Pakistan or its independence. On 12 August 1947, in identical telegrams to the Government of India and Pakistan, the Prime Minister of Kashmir offered a Standstill Agreement 'on all matters on which there exists at present an understanding with the British government'. On 15 August 1947, the Foreign Secretary of Pakistan conveyed the acceptance whereas the reply from India stated: 'Government of India would be glad if you or some other minister duly authorized could fly to Delhi for negotiated Standstill Agreement.'[13]

No agreement was concluded between the state of Jammu and Kashmir and India. Instead the state was advised to seek the cooperation of Sheikh Abdullah and take steps to introduce a responsible government. The state's Prime Minister retorted that there was no responsible government even in India as no elections had been held in India after it became independent.[14]

On 15 October Mehar Chand Mahajan, the Prime Minister of the state declared: 'Kashmir will become Switzerland of the East with friendly relation with both India and Pakistan.'[15] The Maharaja appointed Bakshi Tek Chand, a retired judge of the Punjab High Court, to draft the Constitution of the state.

For various reasons into which we need not go, the Maharaja's understanding with Pakistan was on shaky grounds. The Kashmir Muslim Conference in its session in Srinagar reversed the decision of its counterpart in Jammu and passed a resolution in favour of accession to Pakistan.[16]

In order to neutralize this decision and in response to the pressure of the Government of India, the Maharaja released Sheikh Abdullah from detention on 29 September 1947. Two representatives of Pakistan, Mohammad Taseer and Sheikh Sadiq Hassan, came to Srinagar to persuade Abdullah to take immediate steps to accede to Pakistan. Taseer threatened 'to use other means' if Abdullah did not agree. Abdullah, however, agreed to visit Pakistan after his scheduled visit to Delhi where he had convened a meeting of the working committee of AISPC of which he had been elected President during his detention.[17]

In Delhi, Sheikh Abdullah was received at the airport by Prime Minister Nehru, breaking all protocol, and was given a guard of honour. He was treated as the Prime Minister's personal guest. At the Prime Minister's house, the Sheikh told a press conference, 'Kashmir's future is to be decided by its people and not by the Maharaja. Till people get freedom from Maharaja they cannot take any decision.'

Sheikh Abdullah noted the contrast between the treatment he received in India and the threat delivered by Pakistani representatives. Besides, Pakistan radio had unleashed propaganda against him for the views he had expressed in the press conference.[18]

Pakistan's dilemma was that it could neither trust Abdullah, who was opposed to the Two Nations theory, nor the Maharaja, whose links with the Hindu right were no more a secret. Its relations with the latter were further strained after it started violations of the Standstill Agreement and stopping of supplies of petrol, cloth, and food for which it was the only source as the state's road link with the outside world passed through Pakistan.

Meanwhile anti-Muslim riots started in Jammu for which Mahatma Gandhi said that 'Maharaja as the absolute ruler could not be absolved of the responsibility. He should either abdicate or remain only a titular head and transfer power to the people.'[19]

Later, riots started in the Muslim majority parts of Jammu against Hindus and Sikhs, partly as a reaction to the anti-Muslim riots in other parts of the region and partly as an extension of the adjoining West Punjab riots.

While the state government was in correspondence with Pakistan over the troubled situation in the Jammu region bordering Pakistan, and Jinnah invited the prime minister of the state, on 20 October, to Karachi to discuss the matter,[20] tribesmen from Pakistan launched a full-scale attack on Kashmir, armed and organized by Pakistan's army. The Maharaja sent a contingent of his armed forces under the command of Brigadier Rajendra Singh to face the invasion at Uri. But all of them were eliminated by the invaders who had numerical superiority. Apart from their sacrifice, the martyrdom of two National Conference leaders, Mir Maqbool Sherwani and Master Abdul Aziz, who resisted the raiders and tried to mislead them at Baramulla about the way to Srinagar, was extremely useful in causing a crucial delay in the march of the raiders and to capture Srinagar airport before Indian forces could land there.

When the raiders reached the outskirts of Srinagar, the Maharaja sought the help of the Indian army. The Governor General replied that it could not be done as long as the state was not part of the Indian Union. He was also advised to share power with the National Conference.

Mehar Chand Mahajan and Sheikh Abdullah went to Delhi. Mahajan told Nehru, 'Take accession and give whatever power you want to the popular party but the army must fly to Srinagar this evening. Otherwise I will go and negotiate terms with Jinnah.' Nehru's reaction, in Mahajan's own words was:

> The Prime Minister flew into a rage and told me to go out. Just as I was getting out, Sheikh Abdullah, who was staying in Prime Minister's House and overhearing the talks, sent a slip to the Prime Minister. He read it and said that what I was saying was also the view of Sheikh Sahib and his attitude completely changed.[21]

The Instrument of Accession was signed by the Maharaja on 26 October 1947 under the pressure of popular leadership. Voluntary accession of an overwhelming Muslim majority state of Jammu and Kashmir against the background of communal frenzy and holocaust in the subcontinent, divided on communal lines was a monumental ideological, political, diplomatic, constitutional, and moral triumph for India in which, above all, Nehru had played the major role.

The Government of India was, however, committed to decide the question of accession in case of any state where the question was in dispute in accordance with the wishes of the people. By this logic India rejected the decision of the Nawab of Junagarh to accede to Pakistan and of the Nizam of Hyderabad to remain independent and annexed both the states. It, therefore, referred the matter of Kashmir's accession to India to the Security Council. There is abundant evidence from Pakistani sources that it was not prepared for a plebiscite to decide the future of the state from 1947 to 1953. Jinnah rejected the offer of the Governor General of India Lord Mountbatten on 1 November 1947 to decide the Kashmir issue through a plebiscite but offered to exchange Kashmir with Junagarh. India could not do so without reference to the people of the two states.[22] A British scholar, Alastair Lamb, engaged by Pakistan to lobby its case, concedes that 'with the memories of horrors of tribal raid fresh in the minds of people and Sheikh Abdullah's prestige intact, Pakistan could not afford to lose even that part of the state it had occupied'.[23]

Meanwhile, the Maharaja-Abdullah rift continued over the extent of sharing of power. The Maharaja insisted on adopting the Mysore model which had two schedules—one reserved for the ruler, the other for the popular ministry. He also wanted his nominee Mehar Chand Mahajan, as the Dewan, to preside over the cabinet meetings. Ultimately, Abdullah had his way. The Maharaja, under pressure from the Government of India, agreed to install a popular ministry headed by Sheikh Abdullah in March 1948.

But the tussle between the Maharaja and the Sheikh continued over the role of the Dewan, who eventually had to leave, over the reserved powers of the Maharaja, which, too, were withdrawn and also over the day to day working of the administration. This tussle added to the popularity of the Sheikh in the Kashmir Valley. The Maharaja sent his complaints to Sardar Patel and Sheikh Abdullah to Pandit Nehru. Patel and Nehru resolved their disputes.

At one stage, the Maharaja, in his letter to Patel on 31 January 1948, even threatened to withdraw the accession, though he left the entire matter to Patel 'personally'. Patel forwarded the letter to Nehru who in his reply on

9 February 1948 said that the idea of cancellation of accession is completely wrong. 'That will only lead to trouble for him and for us.'[24]

Similarly, the Sheikh in his interview to foreign correspondents (of *New Statesman, United Press of America,* and *Observer*) on 14 April 1949 proposed the idea of an independent Kashmir to be guaranteed by India, Pakistan, and the UN. Later he retracted this statement and clarified that he was merely thinking aloud. He said it was wrong to equate India with Pakistan. Nehru agreed that the Sheikh had adopted such an approach to neutralize the influence of Pakistan on the Muslims of Kashmir and that 'he is not a clear thinker and he goes astray as many of our politicians do'.[25]

The people of Jammu had been disillusioned with the Maharaja due to his wavering stand on accession and had hailed Sheikh Abdullah for rescuing the state from the tribal raid and for accession to India. But the Sheikh merely aspired to remain a hero of Kashmiri nationalism and did not function as a leader of the entire state. He never had a base in Jammu and did not trust any of the local leaders. Whenever somebody approached him for any administrative or political matter he would direct him to Bakshi Ghulam Mohammad whom he had entrusted with Jammu affairs. He in turn would direct him to one of his assistants S.K. Raina nick-named as Viceroy of Jammu, as he was too busy with his responsibilities as Deputy Prime Minister and Home Minister. Thus Jammu's political and administrative affairs were dealt with by a low-ranking Kashmiri bureaucrat.

In my first meeting with Nehru, I drew his attention to the growing regional tension in the state and warned him of its serious consequences. He told me that according to the then prevailing arrangement, the head of the government was from Kashmir while the Maharaja who belonged to Jammu would be head of the state. 'It should', he said 'satisfy both the regions'.

I told him that, under this arrangement, political power would be exercised by a Kashmiri leader while the people of Jammu would get an impression that a person from their region was a constitutional head, without power, living in a palace inaccessible to them. I pleaded for an arrangement whereby political power could be equitably shared by all regions of the state. Nehru warned that the removal of the Maharaja might upset what he called, 'stable instability' and suggested that the existing system be given a trial. I asserted that it would not work for long as the Maharaja and Abdullah were not even on speaking terms.

Meanwhile, the Jammu National Conference passed a formal resolution demanding the termination of the institution of monarchy and immediate abdication of the Maharaja. The resolution was endorsed by a meeting of the prominent citizens of Jammu. It strengthened my case in my next meeting with Nehru. Maybe this fact also contributed to the abdication of Maharaja Hari Singh in June 1949. His son Karan Singh took his place as Regent. After a prolonged controversy over his power, he was elected by the state constituent assembly as Sadar-e-Riyasat in 1952, as the head of the state was called on the pattern of Governors in other states of India.

When talks on centre-state relations started and Sheikh Abdullah demanded autonomy for the state, I intervened and met Nehru on 14 April 1952. While supporting autonomy for the state, I demanded that its logic should be extended further by conceding autonomy to the regions. I was also able to persuade Abdullah to accept my proposal. Eventually Nehru and Abdullah announced at a joint press conference on 24 July 1952 that 'when the constitution of the state would be framed, it would provide for regional autonomy'.

This decision could not be implemented immediately. Meanwhile power remained confined with Kashmiri leaders. For the top leadership of the ruling National Conference, including its President, Vice President, General Secretary and Treasurer continued to be from the Kashmir region. Moreover, the power was used arbitrarily and no dissent was tolerated. The system was totally regimented as government officers were nominated as office-bearers of the National Conference and vice versa.

The working of the government was not any better in the Valley either. But the Sheikh could arouse popular sentiment by claiming that he brought 'azadi' to Kashmir after four centuries of slavery to outside rulers (Mughals, Afghans, Sikhs, and Dogras), as if people were now ruled by a Kashmiri king. Neither he nor the people had, for a while, any concept of 'azadi' in the sense of democratic freedom. Termination of monarchy and radical land reforms too earned him some popularity. But suppression of democratic freedom gradually had an adverse impact. The first general election was held in the state in 1951. In the Valley no one had the courage to contest as an opposition candidate. In Jammu, the nomination papers of all except two opposition candidates were rejected and the two who contested could not win.

For want of any democratic outlet, the first voice of dissent of a senior National Conference leader G.M. Karra, who was sidelined, expressed itself in the pro-Pakistan slogan of his newly formed People's Conference, though he still claimed to be secular and a Gandhian. In order to steal his thunder the Sheikh made some anti-India noises. Referring to that, Nehru wrote to Abdullah on 2 May 1952, 'You have delivered several speeches during the last fortnight ... my reaction has been one of pain and distress. ... This would harm the cause you and I have at heart. I have decided to remain silent.'[26]

In Jammu, discontent found expression in the form of the Jana Sangh-supported Praja Parishad, a coalition of the loyalists of the Maharaja, disgruntled landlords, and Hindu communal elements against which the Sheikh could arouse Kashmiri sentiment. In Ladakh, Head Lama Kishok Bakula, protested against the 'Srinagar-dominated administration' which might revive 'spiritual longings of the people for a union with their spiritual home Tibet'.[27]

I presented this picture to Nehru and also showed him a copy of an order that the Deputy Commissioner of Doda district had issued, on a visit to Kishtwar, dismissing the tehsil committee of the National Conference and appointing another committee. I asked him, 'Can such a regimented state remain a part of a democratic India?' Nehru in his reply said, 'I am aware of Sheikh Sahib's weaknesses. But our entire Kashmir policy revolves around his personality. Avoid confrontation with him and try to influence him.'

When I broached the subject with the Sheikh, he cited the example of the Soviet Union where this system was working successfully. The Communists had exercised great influence on the National Conference. Its manifesto *New Kashmir* is a communist draft. In its Foreword the Sheikh paid tributes to the Soviet Union where principles enshrined in *New Kashmir* had worked. At that time communists were champions of all regional identities all over India.

I met B.P.L. Bedi, Communist Party of India (CPI) in-charge of Kashmir affairs, and Comrade Sundarayya, leader of CPI in Parliament, and asked them about possible consequences of regional tensions in the state. They frankly admitted that their policy was to widen the regional divide between Kashmir and Jammu as that would encourage the urge for independence in the Kashmir Valley, which would be turned into an arsenal for revolutionary movements in the rest of the country. I reported these facts to Nehru.

During his meeting with Loy Henderson, the then American ambassador in India, Sheikh Abdullah reportedly sought American support for independence. This was confirmed when Henderson's papers were declassified. Thereafter, the American statesman Adlai Stevenson visited Kashmir and stayed there for three days and had prolonged talks with the Sheikh. That completely disillusioned the Communists and created doubts in Delhi about the Sheikh's intentions. Nehru, however, discounted the conspiracy theory, and said so to Chester Bowles, the American ambassador to India.[28]

Nehru invited Abdullah to Delhi to guide him for talks with the Pakistani Prime Minister in their scheduled meeting at the Commonwealth Conference in London. Sheikh Abdullah expressed his inability to leave Kashmir in view of the political tension prevailing there. Thereupon, Maulana Azad, in his letter to Abdullah on 5 July 1953, assured him that the Government of India was willing to declare that 'the Special Status of Kashmir will be made permanent'. Abdullah, in his reply observed, 'If such a declaration had been made at an appropriate time, it would have undoubtedly strengthened our hands and majority of masses would have favoured accession to India.'

More facts need not be cited to explain the reasons that led to the final rupture in the age-old friendship between Nehru and Abdullah and Kashmir's emotional relations with India on 9 August 1953 when Sheikh Abdullah was dismissed and put under detention. *The New York Times* pertinently reported, 'Sheikh Abdullah by leaning towards independence has strengthened his personal support which appeared to be falling off.'[29]

Relations between Nehru and Abdullah were not completely cut off after the latter's incarceration. Abdullah congratulated Nehru on his escape in an accident near Nagpur and asked for the clarification of a statement by Nehru in Parliament that mistakes committed by Abdullah had given him a jolt and yet his affection had not lessened.

Nehru in his reply on 8 April 1955 thanked Abdullah for his message of congratulation and offered a detailed explanation of what he had said in Parliament. He wrote:

I begged of you not to take any step that might worsen the situation during my absence from India but I had contrary reports which induced Maulana Azad to visit Kashmir. He was treated with active discourtesy and his advice was rejected.

I communicated with you by letter, telephone and telegram begging you to come to Delhi. In the course of your reply, you indicated that there was not much point in our carrying on correspondence. You also did not think it worthwhile to come to Delhi. This made me feel completely helpless and I became a passive spectator of the march of events.[30]

Nehru retained contacts with Abdullah's sons and his friends like Maulana Massoodi and even recommended Massoodi's name to Bakshi for renomination to Parliament (which he did not do). Abdullah also had contacts with Rajagopalachari, Jayaprakash Narayan, and many Gandhians and socialists in India. Thus his umbilical cord with India was not completely cut off.

I was one of the first persons in the country from outside the Valley who initiated a campaign to mobilize support to protest against the action of the Government of India against the Sheikh. It surprised him in jail as he had not treated me well. When I met Nehru, he asked me, 'You were a critic of the Sheikh, why are you criticizing action against him?' I replied, 'I was critical of him because he was not a democrat. But I did not want him to be removed undemocratically. If my criticism had been heeded, there might not have been the need to remove him. Moreover, now he represents almost the entire people of Kashmir region whom we cannot write off.' I was more critical of Bakshi Ghulam Mohammad who had succeeded him. He not only inherited a regimented system and strengthened it but used lavish temptations to win over the majority of the cabinet ministers, legislators, and a substantial section of National Conference cadres, though some of them changed their loyalty, from Sheikh to Bakshi out of conviction. Nehru argued, 'We gambled on Kashmir which we cannot afford to lose. Unfortunately Kashmir politics revolves around personalities and there is no material for democracy there.'

An incident which had a great impact on the Sheikh's relations with me took place on the opening day of the trial against him in 1957. As he entered the court room we wished each other. The Inspector General of Police (IGP) objected to it and ordered the policemen there to 'teach me a lesson'. I was taken into custody and beaten mercilessly. The issue was raised in Parliament, and by Pakistan in the Security Council. It said, 'When a person of the stature of Balraj Puri can be beaten, the condition of the common man can be imagined.' It demanded a special session of the Council to discuss the situation. An officer of the Prime Minister's Office brought a letter of regret from Nehru with a verbal request not to pursue the matter further. I was also told that the Government of India would not offer any defence to Pakistan's complaint in the Security Council. I agreed not to pursue the matter. This incident made my access to the Sheikh in the sub-jail attached with the special court much easier and endeared me to him further.

I had long talks with him on all aspects of the Kashmir problem. I discovered that he still had a soft corner for Nehru.

After doing my bit for softening their attitude towards each other and discussing many problems facing the state, I raised the subject of the final solution for the Kashmir problem. He, of course, stood for independent Kashmir. I asked him how he would defend it and added, 'If you are forced to choose between Indian army and Pakistani army, hypothetically what would be your preference?' He tried to avoid a reply but when I persisted, he said, 'We have quite a good experience of the Indian army. But if Pakistani army comes, its Punjabi soldiers would not spare any Kashmiri woman, and the next generation will not be of Kashmiris.'

Next I asked, 'What about foreign affairs, will you export all Kashmiri talent to run your foreign embassies?' He said, 'If I settle all matters at your level, what will I discuss with Nehru?'

I met Nehru and told him that in my assessment there was room for a settlement with the Sheikh. He might have verified my assessment from other sources. The Sheikh was released and invited to Delhi in May 1964 where he stayed at the Prime Minister's house.

The Sheikh and his team went to Pakistan with Nehru's consent with a formula of India, Pakistan, and Kashmir confederation. General Ayub Khan, Pakistan's President, predictably rejected the formula. Due to the sudden demise of Nehru, Sheikh had to cut short his Pakistan visit and return to Delhi. I received him at the airport. He said, 'Take me straight to Nehru's Samadhi'.

We visited the Samadhi. Standing there like a statue tears rolled down on his cheeks. On our journey back, he told me, 'Had I learnt that Panditji's death was so near, I need not have gone to Pakistan as I had settled the issue with him'.

On his return to Srinagar, he told a mammoth public condolence meeting that the greatest Kashmiri and friend of Kashmir was no more.

Had Nehru lived some days more, he would have settled the Kashmir problem almost permanently.

Notes

1. Jawaharlal Nehru (1934-35), *Glimpses of World History*, New Delhi: Penguin Books. Reprint 2004, p. 25 and 477.
2. Sheikh Abdullah (1985), *Atash-e-Chinar: Autobiography*, Srinagar: Ali Mohammad and Sons, p. 333.
3. S. Gopal, (1982), *Selected Works of Jawaharlal Nehru*, Vol. 15, Series I, New Delhi: Orient Longman Ltd., p. 388.
4. Ibid., p. 390.
5. Pyarelal, *Mahatma Gandhi: The Last Phase*, Vol. II, Ahmedabad: Navjivan Publishing House, p. 358.
6. Balraj Puri (2005), *JP on Jammu and Kashmir*, New Delhi: Gyan Books, pp. 26-7.
7. Pyarelal, p. 342.
8. *The Hindu*, 17 June 1947.
9. Pyarelal, p. 342.
10. *Khidmat*, Srinagar, 11 July 1947.
11. Allen Campbell Johnson (1951), *Mission with Mountbatten*, London: R. Hale, p. 120.
12. Mehar Chand Mahajan (1963), *Looking Back: Autobiography of Mehar Chand Mahajan*, p. 265.
13. Lakhanpal, *Essential Documents on Kashmir*, New Delhi, p. 45.
14. Ranbir, Press Statement, Jammu 21 October 1947.
15. *Khidmat*, Srinagar, 17 October 1947.
16. Ranbir, Press Statement, 25 July 1947.
17. Sheikh Abdullah (1985), p. 395.
18. Ibid.
19. Pyarelal, p. 2.
20. Quoted in Jyoti Bhushan Das Gupta (1968), *Jammu and Kashmir*, The Hague, p. 82.

21. Mehar Chand Mahajan (1963), *Looking Back: Autobiography of Mehar Chand Mahajan*, p. 277.
22. Pyarelal, p. 342.
23. Alastair Lamb (1991), *Kashmir: Disputed Legacy*, Oxford Books, p. 166.
24. Sardar Patel's Correspondence, 1945–50, Vol. 1, p. 157.
25. *The Hindu*, 19 May 1949.
26. *Selected Works of Jawaharlal Nehru*, (1996), Vol. 18, p. 390.
27. *Amrita Bazar Patrika*, 18 March 1952.
28. *Selected Works of Jawaharlal Nehru*, (1996), Vol. 18, Series 2, pp. 429-30.
29. Quoted in S. Vashisht, *Sheikh Abdullah: Then and Now*, p. 96.
30. *Selected Works of Jawaharlal Nehru*, (2000), Vol. 28, p. 354.

INDER MALHOTRA

7

Understanding Nehru's Policies

In pursuit of the theme as to what was witnessed in the whole period of formation of India into a nation-state, I intend to concentrate on a fundamental paradox in this land of paradoxes. Let me try and explain what the paradox is. Here is Jawaharlal Nehru, who I think is the greatest of all Indians of our times, next only to the Mahatma Gandhi. The Mahatma was the liberator of this country and Nehru its modernizer. As prime minister of independent India for the first seventeen and highly formative years, Nehru disproved those who thought that the huge landmass, so diverse, so bewilderingly complex that India could not last in one piece. Jawaharlal Nehru functioning on the background of the trauma of Partition that accompanied Independence, welded India into one nation. He had to face many challenges. He was the founder of Indian democracy, Indian federalism, a great respecter of Parliament, basically the builder of Indian democracy, and the founder of a modern state on certain principles of equality and tolerance. Yet this man today and, for quite some years has been a target of a relentless and remorseless campaign of denigration. It is a tawdry campaign to somehow tarnish his image. Indeed it is no exaggeration to say that it is 'open season' on Nehru.

There are several sources on this and his detractors have various motivations. Surprisingly, the environmentalists are among them. At an environmental seminar some years ago, I was horrified to hear an angry young man declare that Nehru was to the environment exactly 'what Nathuram Godse was to Mahatma Gandhi'. So in the tea-break I asked him how he came to this conclusion. He gave the example of the Bhakra-Nangal dam and said that it had completely ruined the environment. I asked him if he had any idea when it was built, whether he knew who built it and when the scheme was first thought of. I told him that it was thought of thirty years before Nehru—in the British days. The man who built it was the same man who built the Tennessee Valley dam in the United States. It was on that dam and not on the Napier in Russia that Bhakra was designed. At that time every country in the world was building dams. Dams are being built here as well as in China even today. So I told him to have some sense of proportion. He was a bit noncommittal. This young man might have been talking about the environment but basically, he was airing the views of the young people in India, especially those belonging to the upper middle class and relatively affluent families who unfortunately know very little about modern Indian history. They somehow convince themselves that if Nehru and his foolish socialist policies were not there, the joys of globalization and liberalization would have been available to them long ago. One of them told me that they were 'deprived' for a long time. When I asked him what they were deprived of, he replied that they had only the Ambassador car and the Fiat. The imported cars like BMW, Honda, etc. were not available. I asked him whether he realized that even today there are nearly half a billion people who are poor and some of them do not even get two square meals a day. Are they not deprived? These people have had some correctives from the global meltdown that has exposed the underbelly of globalization. They, as well as the other champions of free market, have suddenly realized and become defenders of massive bailouts of the free enterprise by the governments.

In Nehru's case, the whole idea of planned economy to accelerate development and overcome the gap between the rich and the poor began as far back as 1938, when Indian National Congress in Karachi passed a resolution drafted by him asking for a National Planning Committee. The members of this committee nominated by the Congress included J.R.D. Tata, G.D. Birla, and some very distinguished economists. I looked up the history of the Congress and found that this resolution, though drafted by Nehru was moved by the Mahatma. Privately, Gandhiji had told Nehru that he would do it because if the younger man moved it, then it would certainly evoke opposition. That is exactly what happened. Four years later, Gandhiji declared Nehru to be his political heir calling him the 'Jewel of India' and proclaiming that the future of the country would be safe in his hands. Predictably, other leaders such as Sardar Vallabhbhai Patel, Rajaji, Rajendra Prasad, and others expressed to the Mahatma their reservations on the ground of Nehru's socialism. Gandhiji's reply was 'Nehru would speak my language'. To be honest, Nehru did not speak Gandhi's language. He did precisely what he thought was good for the country, such as industrialization. He went ahead with his own ideas, whereas the Mahatma would have preferred India to be a very loose confederation of half a million autonomous and semi-independent villages, Nehru wanted a federal Indian state with a strong industrial and technological base. Irrespective of their varied approaches, Nehru fully vindicated Gandhiji's faith in him.

Nehru used the expression 'controlling of the commanding heights of economy'. He was not the only one to do so. Nye Bevan was the first to use it in Britain. Social democrats of France, Germany, and other European countries were using it. It was also being used in Latin America. It may be remembered that for Nehru, socialism meant egalitarianism, it meant mixed economy, it meant putting agriculture totally in private hands. He was always for collective action when necessary, however, he always took care to uphold the dignity of the individual. Yet there are some people who go to the absurd length of calling his policies 'Stalinist'. To say all this is not to deny that, even in his lifetime, his policies were most suitable in the context and the circumstances of those days and even later. They had started turning into what Rajaji called '*license permit quota raj*' around the time he passed away. I think he was also conscious of it. I do not know and cannot predict what he would have done had he lived longer. He was not a static but a dynamic person. I must also say that if he had not built the basic foundation of industry, technology and science it would not have been possible to build any superstructure. Unfortunately, the reckless and, sometimes ill-considered expansion of the public sector, enactment of laws like the Monopolies and Restrictive Trade Practices Act, the Urban Land Ceiling Act, and so on, are all products of an era after his time, largely, I am afraid, under the watch of his daughter Indira Gandhi. But the youngsters would know little of what a privilege and joy it was to live under Nehru's civilized rule. In his time, equality before the law was the norm. He respected dissent. He had to struggle with enormous dignity against President Rajendra Prasad to get the Hindu Code Bill passed. He faced enormous resistance within his own party. But whatever he did or fought for, he stuck to the democratic method. Democracy for him was an article of faith. No wonder he saw to it that the very first election in 1952 took place on the basis of adult suffrage and not limited franchise. To the youngsters, my advice is that, before denouncing Nehru, please try and read him.

Let me confess that I belong to a generation that can be called 'Nehru's children'. We were captivated by his magical personality, by his phenomenal popularity with the masses, by his charisma and, above all, by his inspiring vision of India. We were educated in schools, colleges, and universities but I can say that we learnt a lot more from the three classics—*Glimpses of World History*, *Discovery of India*, and his *An Autobiography*. The Nehru era was an age of hope and excitement, something that I do not see around today. Certainly, there has been a great deal of achievement, there is no doubt about it. Our Gross Domestic Product (GDP) was much smaller compared to what it is today. Our military power was very much less than what we can boast of today. But I do say that, at that time, we walked tall.

Let me now turn to the second and, more vicious source of systematic demonization of Jawaharlal Nehru. Incidentally, of the tall world leaders of that era, few are remembered so fondly and with such nostalgia as Jawaharlal Nehru is. But there is a group of people that are full of hatred for Nehru and his philosophy and legacy. Ideologically driven, they are determined to dismantle his greatest achievement—the founding and nurturing of the modern, democratic, and secular Indian society and Indian State, committed to protecting and preserving this country's plurality and its inclusiveness. To be fair, the practice of Nehruvian secularism, even in his time, and certainly after his lifetime, has not always been perfect. In the noble venture of ensuring equality before the law and eliminating divisiveness on the basis of religion, caste, or region, Nehru did not succeed fully. But, to borrow his phrase (used in a different context), he did succeed substantially. The secularism that he built, therefore, has proved strong enough to withstand the most virulent assaults on it. Neither the hysteria over Ram Janambhoomi nor the demolition of the Babri Masjid nor the ranting against minority appeasement, against votebank politics, and against 'softness on jihadi terrorism' has worked for those who want to get rid of secularism completely. In fact, if the Hindutva hotheads have failed to make India a Hindu Pakistan, the credit primarily goes to Jawaharlal Nehru. The more these people are frustrated in their nefarious efforts, the greater becomes their anger against the man. In this context, what an irony it is that the voters' overwhelming verdict in the latest election is for moderation, stability, total avoidance of religious hatred and violence, peace, and stability. Even some leaders of the Hindu right are privately admitting that the Hindutva card has let them down. The verdict is but an endorsement of Nehru's legacy.

Having said this, let me turn to the other side of the coin. As Saint Augustine said, 'No one can rule guiltlessly'. Nor is any human being, Nehru included, Gandhiji included, infallible. Of course, Nehru made mistakes, some of them serious, and these need to be discussed openly. However, leaving aside the ranting and raving of the habitual Nehru-bashers, let us concentrate on what the really serious critics have picked on and, rightly. These two issues are China and Kashmir. It is said that these two should be reckoned among his failings. So the argument goes. Here also, there is some irony because foreign policy was Nehru's special arena in which he was past master and the role that he played as an actor on the world stage was the envy of his counterparts across the world, certainly in the Third World. Yet, it was in this era that these two failures lay. Nehru's policy of non-alignment was nothing short of a stroke of genius in the context of the Cold War between the two power blocs frozen in mutual hostility and bitterness. It bears mentioning that Nehru enunciated this policy of non-alignment six days after he joined the Viceroy's Executive Council as the Head of the Indian Government. India was not independent then. Nobody knew whether the successors to the British Raj will be one government or two. But the interesting thing is that when the Muslim League came into the Interim Government they said or did nothing to oppose what Nehru had proposed. It is a different matter, of course, that some of his disciples later on converted what he devised as a doctrine and a policy to safeguard India's security and supreme interest into a *mantra* to be chanted in season and out of season. I do remember a particular occasion when he had to tell the Parliament that he could not be non-aligned against himself.

Critics of the China policy also have a valid point. But I am afraid they are profoundly wrong in choosing the basis on which they are blaming the great man. For example, all of them have been saying consistently and persistently that Nehru was naïve, that he was taken in by China's false protestations. Some have even accused him of being the person who coined the slogan 'Hindi Chini bhai bhai'. He did not invent it. This was done by Harindranath Chattopadhyay, a poet and actor. He had gone to China as part of an unofficial delegation where he coined this phrase. Although Nehru erred on other things as well, naivete and gullibility were not among his weaknesses. There is plenty of evidence of this. G. Parthasarathy, who was India's Ambassador to China from 1958 to 1961, maintained a private diary. It never saw the light of day until his son decided to publish excerpts from it. I will quote one single entry dated 18 March 1958.

> I went to see Panditji at 11.00 pm for my final and most important briefing. As I sat down opposite him at his huge and beautiful desk, Panditji said—'So GP, what has the Foreign Office told you? Hindi Chini, bhai bhai? Don't you believe it. I don't trust the Chinese one bit. Despite Panchsheel and all that, the Chinese are arrogant, devious, hypocritical and thoroughly unreliable. In fact, they have deliberately chosen to be anti-Indian. Your brief from me, therefore, is to be extremely vigilant about the Chinese intentions, policies and actions towards us. All your telegrams should be marked TOP SECRET and sent to me alone.'

We have heard everybody blame him for being a bad judge of men and, therefore, having ruined himself and the country by trusting Krishna Menon so much. So, on that background, this is what he said to G. Parthasarathy, 'You should also be very careful in your meetings and discussions with Krishna. Don't let him see any of your telegrams. All three of us share a common world view. But Krishna allows his thinking and assessments to be clouded on this matter of our relations with China merely because China is a Communist country.' These could not have been the words of a man who was naïve.

Four years earlier, an official goodwill mission had gone to China led by Panditji's sister, Vijaylakshmi Pandit. Two of its members were very distinguished editors, Frank Moraes and M. Chalapati Rao. Both of them told me then (off the record, of course), and later Frank Moraes put it in his book *Witness to an Era* that Panditji had told them that there was a basic conflict between China and India which extended all along 'Asia's spine'.

Tibet played a very important part in this escalating conflict. The Chinese have not been able to pacify Tibet all these years till today. In 1959 they were shaken by the major uprising at that time when the Dalai Lama fled from Lhasa and India decided to give him asylum. This is what had aggravated the relationship. Until then, the Chinese had not said very much on the border issue. They drew blood for the first time in Ladakh. In an atmosphere of bitter rancour, the public opinion in this country got so inflamed that nobody could control it. Any kind of attempt to compromise on the border issue became impossible. Moreover, several critics, even today, feel that Nehru should not have allowed the Chinese to occupy Tibet and thus remove the buffer between the two Asian powers. How could he have sent an Indian expeditionary force into the wilderness of Tibet to take on the People's Liberation Army that had won the thirty-year civil war in their country and then fought McArthur in Korea? As it happened, during the rather short first Kashmir war in 1947–8 with the Pakistanis, where a ceasefire had come into effect on 1 January 1949, we had found that we did not even have enough jeeps. So what could we have done to counter China as far as Tibet is concerned at a time when no power in the world was prepared to do so, not the British, nor the Americans, nor anybody else and certainly not the Russians?

The second thing that his detractors say is that, in 1954, the agreement between India and China on the Tibet region of China regarding trade, etc. should never have been signed. What else could Nehru do? Purshottam Mehra is a very distinguished scholar on the China question. He has given a definitive answer to this. He has said that, even the British, at a time when British power could interfere with and perhaps dominate when necessary, to the anger of the Tibetans, took care to pay lip service to China's ultimate control of Tibet. By 1954 the power equation had changed radically and dramatically. So where did Nehru go wrong? My submission is that his mistake was not in what he did. He tried his best to see that Tibetan autonomy was preserved. The Chinese entered into an agreement with the Dalai Lama on 17 May 1951, which they had no intention of honouring. By

1959, it had been reduced to tatters. But Nehru's mistake was that while signing this agreement he refrained from insisting that the border issue must be settled simultaneously. Sadly, he did not take Sir Girija Shankar Bajpai's advice to this effect. Instead he allowed himself to be persuaded that since the border was not an issue, it must not be raised during the negotiations.

In the east, we had the McMahon Line drawn at the Simla Convention of 1914 at a time when the Chinese delegate was also present. It is a different matter that he did not sign the convention though he initiated it. The Chinese did not ratify it either. But Tibet did and the line existed. Hence, Nehru's position: 'The McMahon Line is our border, map or no map'. But in regard to the western sector there was no agreement of any kind. Unfortunately, Indian attention, including Sardar Patel's famous letter to Nehru on 7 November 1950 just thought of the border as the McMahon Line. There was no thinking beyond the McMahon Line and in particular, no attention was paid to the western border. It was, then, by India's acknowledged position, undefined. This was surely a major error.

As for the reasons that led to the 1962 debacle, Nehru's great mistake was that somehow he convinced himself that despite the entire tension, angry notes, the Chinese publications of Nehru and his philosophy of Tibet and such abusive documents he did not perceive a big threat. Border clashes or skirmishes between patrols were minor matters. What his logic was I also fail to understand and it never occurred to him nor did anybody point out to him that the Chinese could conduct limited, well-planned, well-calibrated, and punitive exercise which they eventually did. In retrospect, we have hugely exaggerated the 1962 debacle. A very small section of Indian and Chinese armies were involved on bleak heights. The border war lasted only a month. But we allowed ourselves to be totally demoralized. Our real misfortune, in my view, was the unfortunate fact that, at no stage, was there anyone among Nehru's advisers—civilian, military, or political— who could engage with him intellectually, question his formulations or, at least, argue with him against his judgement. 'Panditji knows best' was the prevailing doctrine.

On the Kashmir issue, the criticism of Nehru is even more untenable. He is constantly censured for having taken the issue to the United Nations (UN) and for promising a plebiscite. It has to be known that if we had not taken the matter to the UN, somebody else would have. Britain had been telling us that India and Pakistan should refer the issue jointly to the UN and then they started indicating that if we did not do it, they would do it on their own. That is when, I think we decided, quite wisely, to take the plunge. And we did it under Chapter VI of the UN Charter which deals with threat to peace. I am absolutely certain that, if anybody else would have taken the Kashmir issue to the UN, they would have done it under the mandatory Chapter VII under which the UN could have decided to post its troops on both sides of the Line of Control. When Nehru took this issue to Gandhiji, he approved of the decision to go to the UN. On the relevant file, there are some corrections in the Mahatma's own hand. Another flaw in our understanding is our inability to look at the context. We always believe that each issue is an issue in isolation or indeed exists in a watertight compartment. It has no linkage with anything else. All the writings and speeches on Kashmir have rarely shown awareness of the fact that the Kashmir issue was vitally and somewhat dangerously linked with Hyderabad. People do not even seem to remember that. Jinnah was not being foolish in asserting that in relation to an accession to either of the two dominions by any Indian princely state, the word of the ruler was final. The British endorsed it and said that this was the position, though there were other considerations which had to be weighed. Nehru contested this position very strongly and said that the Instrument of Accession could be signed by the ruler but it would have no validity until the people of the state concerned endorsed it. In these circumstances, how could he accept the Kashmir Accession finally on the word of the Maharaja alone and not promise the plebiscite? First, he insisted that the Maharaja should install a popular government which would facilitate the plebiscite. It should be added that Vallabhbhai Patel, the strong-willed leader, was aware from the very beginning of the danger of Hyderabad doing some mischief because he knew what the Pakistani game-plan was. The Pakistani plan was that the Nizam should declare independence, sign a treaty of mutual defence with Pakistan and simultaneously apply for a membership of the British Commonwealth. The Pakistani intermediary for this purpose was Shaukat Hayat Khan. It was through him, as he published ten years later, India sent a feeler to Liaqat Ali Khan that they should leave Hyderabad alone and stop meddling in its affairs, then only would India think of letting Kashmir go to Pakistan. Liaqat rejected the deal out of hand and contemptuously. His argument was that the Muslim majority would come to them anyway. To have the State of Hyderabad in the centre of India as a partner of Pakistan was what they wanted. I would add that people have not realized that we accepted the resolution of 13 August 1948 of the United Nations Commission for India and Pakistan only after the Hyderabad issue was taken care of.

From that follows the second criticism of Nehru that instead of accepting the ceasefire in Kashmir, we could have easily cleared up the Valley. Have the critics checked with the host? Sheikh Abdullah told Jawaharlal Nehru that his following was confined to the Kashmiri people and did not extend to the Punjabi Muslims inhabiting what is now 'Azad Kashmir'. That is how the ceasefire line, now called the Line of Control, was drawn. Assuming that we could have gone right up to the doorstep of Rawalpindi is wrong. The Israelis occupy the whole of Palestine. Have they got either security or settlement?

I would like to conclude by referring to three other people. The first one is Dean Acheson. He was Truman's Secretary of State. In 1949, when Nehru first went there, he found that there was no go with the United States. Yet Acheson writes: 'Nehru and I were not destined to be friends. But India was so important to the world and Nehru so important to India that if he didn't exist, then as Voltaire said of God, we would have to invent him'. So much from an adversary. Second, the Communist Party of India's relations with Nehru were quite bad for a long time though they respected him. Its very own respected member, Hiren Mukherjee, wrote a biography of Nehru and he called it *The Gentle Colossus*. The third person is the no-nonsense man, a thorough sceptic, a prickly person, Nirad C. Chaudhuri. Towards the end, he started calling Nehru 'India's ineffectual angel'. In one of his lesser known writings in *The Illustrated Weekly* of May 1953, he said,

Nehru's leadership is the most important moral force behind the unity of India. He is the leader not of a party but of a people of India taken collectively. He keeps together the government machine and the people. If within India, Nehru is the indispensable link between the governing middle classes and the sovereign people, he is no less the bond between India and the world.

K. NATWAR SINGH

8

A Brief Survey of
Jawaharlal Nehru's Foreign Policy

His life was gentle,
and the elements, so mixed in him
that Nature might stand up
and say to all the world 'This was a man.'
—Shakespeare

This short essay is not a comprehensive or scholarly assessment of
Jawaharlal Nehru's foreign policy. It is a brief and tentative survey in
which I have reflected on a few of his more substantial policy concerns and
preoccupations.

I have been an admirer of Nehru. Yet, I have resisted the temptation to
canonize him or attribute scriptural virtues to his actions, thinking, or to his
grasp of the historical process. That would need a book in itself.

Although Nehru was not an original or incisive thinker, none can deny
his intellectual concentration and moral passion, his intense commitment
to peace and harmony among nation states. The furniture of his mind

combined the traditional and the contemporary. In his character there was no hollowness. He was gifted with a luminous personality, which seldom neglected catering for his persona. He did so with sophistication. He was a poor judge of men, but an exceptionally good judge of the mood of the masses. While addressing huge crowds he could be prolix and didactic. But that did not matter. A vast majority had come to see Panditji.

Nehru's mentor was Gandhi, but he was not a Gandhian in any dogmatic way. He was an idealist who had disdain for the power game, which infected the superpowers and their obedient clients. He had no interest in *realpolitik*.

Nehru followed an independent non-aligned policy, not an episodic one. His most spectacular legacy is the broad national consensus on foreign policy. This consensus has survived for sixty-three years.

He studied history, wrote history, made and shaped history. Yet the ambiguities of history bypassed him. He was shackled by his own version of history. His *weltanschauung* resonated. His authority was derived from various sources from which his character and personality drew strength.

He was certainly not without faults. His understanding of economics was inadequate. In his seventeen years as External Affairs Minister there were no economic or foreign policy planning divisions in the Ministry. He changed India in many ways, but he was perhaps unfamiliar with at least one of Machiavelli's realistic pronouncements on statecraft.

The much denounced Italian wrote, 'There is nothing more difficult to carry out, nor more doubtful of success, nor more dangerous to handle, than to initiate a new order of things.'

If Nehru had not grievously faulted on Kashmir and China he would have gone down as one of the greatest foreign ministers of all time. In these two cases the green lights turned red. His grandson Rajiv Gandhi repaired the China faultiness, not wholly but substantially. But Kashmir remains a troubling bequest. Our relations with China are running into troubled waters. The border issue has not been resolved.

1927–47: Shadow Foreign Minister

Jawaharlal Nehru died on 27 May 1964. Although history has not been kind to him, Jawaharlal Nehru was undoubtedly among the tallest political figures of the twentieth century. He was, by any criteria, a great man. How do we define greatness? The Oxford philosopher Sir Isaiah Berlin

(1909–1997) once said, 'To call someone a great man is to claim that he has intentionally taken a large step, one far beyond the normal capacities of men, in satisfying, or materially affecting, central human interests. ... who permanently and radically alters the outlook and values of a significant body of human beings ... his active intervention makes, what seemed highly improbable, in fact to happen.'

On every count, Nehru emerges with flying colours. He altered and influenced the intellectual, political, and social outlook of a large number of Indians.

While Gandhiji was the moral and ethical guru of Indian National Congress, Nehru provided the intellectual and radical underpinning to the freedom movement.

To my generation, Gandhiji was a remote prophet, to be revered and venerated. Nehru caught our imagination, transformed our way of thinking, and added flair and civility to politics. His courage, brio, love of adventure, and the gambler's instinct (derived from his father), his sophistication, his modernity, and his magnanimity appealed to us. His energy, even his well-rehearsed tantrums excited us. For a while Indian politics took wing.

In March 1926 he and his ailing wife Kamla sailed for Europe. She was suffering from tuberculosis. In those days there was no cure for the disease. Their daughter Indira accompanied her parents. She was eight years old. Nehru was going to England and Europe after fourteen years.

In February 1927, the All India Congress Committee (AICC) asked him to represent it at the International Congress against imperialism being held in Brussels. He was an active participant.

He spoke at the conference on 10 February 1927. As a first address at a significant political event, it was a competent though not an inspiring debut. To the AICC he sent comprehensive and prolix reports. The Congress party had no serious interest in foreign affairs. I think this is a significant event as this conference gave the AICC representative an excellent opportunity to get to know a number of well-known delegates from Britain, the US, Dutch East Indies (Mohd. Hatta who in 1955, became Vice-President of Indonesia), Annam, Korea, Morocco, French North Africa (Arab and Negro), South Africa (both Negro and white labour), Mexico, and Germany. However, there was no follow-up of the various resolutions passed at the conference. Eventually Nehru resigned as its Vice President.

In October 1927, Nehru and his father visited Moscow on the tenth anniversary of the Russian Revolution. He was impressed with the Soviet experiment and on his return wrote a somewhat starry-eyed book on his eight-day visit.

Did his twenty-seven-month stay abroad add up to anything? Yes. He was, in some ways, a different man when he returned. He matured; his level of confidence was further enhanced. He gained fresh insight into the human condition. The contours of his future vision could be discerned. He was bubbling with new ideas. Life's phantasmagoria excited him. His impulsiveness remained. He was gently reprimanded by the Mahatma for this at the 1927 AICC session at Madras. Nevertheless he made his party aware of the reality that there was a world outside India, which the Congress must not neglect.

In 1929 Jawaharlal Nehru was, for the first time elected President of the Indian National Congress, mainly because Gandhi and Motilal Nehru pushed his candidature. Nehru was embarrassed. He said, 'I came out of a trap door.'

In his Presidential address, delivered at Lahore, the youthful leader did something novel. He touched on foreign affairs. Nehru said,

> India today is part of the world movement. Not only China, Turkey and Egypt, but also Russia and other countries of the West are taking part in this movement, and India cannot isolate herself from it. We have our problems, difficult and intricate, and we cannot run away from them and take shelter in the wider problems that affect the world. But if we ignore the world, we do so at our peril.

Between 1930 and 1935 Nehru spent more time in jail than out of it. Prison became a self-created university. He read hundreds of books while a guest of His Majesty's government in various prison cells. Foreign affairs became a passion. He made India's fight against colonialism a world issue. He and his later writings highlighted the evils of colonialism and imperialism in Africa, both north and south of the Sahara. He completed his autobiography in jail and also the massive and gripping work, *Glimpses of World History*. When I was at the UN, several African leaders told me how inspired they were by the freedom struggle led by Gandhi and by Nehru's books.

Nehru was suddenly discharged from Almora jail on 4 September 1935. He flew by KLM to Europe to be with his desperately sick wife Kamla

Nehru. In spite of the best possible medical aid, Kamla Nehru died on 28 February 1936 at the young age of 36.

On the return air journey, with an urn containing Kamla's ashes, Nehru had to spend a night in Rome. A most extraordinary scene was enacted at the airport. The Italian government invited Nehru to meet Italy's Fascist dictator Benito Mussolini (1883–1945). The Chief of Protocol pestered him for an hour, saying that Signor Mussolini was waiting for him. Nehru firmly and politely refused to oblige. He was already a dedicated denouncer of Fascism.

Europe 1938

Most biographers have paid scant attention to this rewarding and worthwhile tour. Nehru sailed for Europe on 2 June 1938.

Nehru was now better known in England. His autobiography, published in 1936, had impressed influential people in England.

On the way to Europe he spent a night in Alexandria as a guest of the Wafd party and its leader Nahas Pasha. Thus a link was established with the Arab world. Nehru was sympathetic to the demand of the Jews for a homeland but did also ask for a fair deal for the Arabs.

On arrival in Europe, Nehru's first call was strife-ridden Spain. He was outraged by the atrocities being committed by General Franco and his Nazi and Fascist supporters. He considered the role of Britain and France as deplorable. He wrote to a leading British newspaper, 'History, long ages from now will remember this infamy and will not forgive them.' The turmoil in his heart and mind was not a passing one. It left scars.

In England he spoke to small, powerful groups to place before them the iniquities of British rule in India. He spoke to the leaders of the Labour Party—C.R. Attlee, Aneurin Bevan, Cripps, and Harold Laski. He heard the appeasement debates in the House of Commons from the visitors' gallery. Chamberlain, the British Prime Minister, made a poor impression on him. Chamberlain's predecessor Stanley Baldwin was the founder of the supine appeasement policy. The British appeared to suffer from unusual apathy. Nehru along with Churchill (they were not to meet till 1953) severely condemned the appeasement of Hitler, who tore up the Treaty of Versailles with impunity. Nehru was not overwhelmed by the leaders of the Labour Party but his getting to know them helped him to understand their political thinking and priorities. They mattered. He also met some Tory politicians and Lord Linlithgow, the Viceroy, who was on leave in England at the time.

Nehru issued a statement on 26 September 1938 on the 'Betrayal of Czechoslovakia'. He ends his statement thus:

> So tomorrow Chamberlain meets Hitler and Mussolini. One was too much for him, what will be his fate with these two strong men? Perhaps Mr. Chamberlain and Monsieur Daladier will agree to everything Hitler says, and then, as another of his great favours, Hitler will consent to postpone war by a few days or weeks. This will indeed be a great triumph and Hitler ought to be hailed then as the prophet of peace. The Nobel Peace Prize might still be awarded to him, though Mr. Chamberlain could be a hot contender.

Who said Jawaharlal Nehru did not have a sense of humour!

Before returning to India, Nehru paid visits to Prague, Budapest, Vienna, and Geneva where the functioning of the League of Nations depressed him no end.

What was the concrete result of this tour? Personally it made Nehru a highly respected Indian leader, who had put the case for Indian independence with skill and in a language that the British understood. He also made it abundantly clear that an independent India would pursue an independent foreign policy. Later he wrote:

> My mind was full of the war coming. I thought of it and spoke of it and wrote about it, and prepared myself mentally for it. I wanted India to take an eager and active part in the mighty conflict, for I felt that high principles would be at stake, and out of this conflict would come great revolutionary changes in India and the world.

These were prophetic words.

Phase Two: From Prisoner to Prime Minister

The Second World War started on 3 September 1939. Nehru was then two months short of his fiftieth birthday. He had to cut his China visit short and return to India. He was the undisputed mass leader next only to Gandhiji in the Congress. On foreign affairs he had the last word.

Between 1940 and 1945 too, he was mostly in prison. The Second World War ended on 8 May 1945. Jawaharlal Nehru along with all Congress Working Committee members was released from prison in

June. Politics went into top gear. Independence was no longer a distant dream. Lord Wavell, the Viceroy, announced the formation of an interim government. Jawaharlal Nehru was invited to be its Vice President. On 2 September 1946, he assumed office, one year and three months after being His Majesty's prisoner. His portfolios were External Affairs and Commonwealth Relations.

In a radio broadcast to the nation on 7 September 1946, Nehru, in general terms put forward the foreign policy framework of his government. We shall take full part in international conferences as a free nation with our own policy and not merely as a satellite of another nation. We hope to develop close and direct contacts with other nations and to co-operate with them in the furtherance of world peace and freedom.

He did not use the word 'non-alignment' but came near enough.

> We propose, as far as possible, to keep away from the power politics of groups, aligned against one another ... The world, in spite of its rivalries and hatreds and inner conflicts, moves inevitably towards closer co-operation and the building up of a world commonwealth. It is for this one world that free India will work, a world in which there is the co-operation of free peoples, and no class or group exploits another.

This declaration of intent was high-minded, idealistic, and novel. It was also simplistic and unrealistic. As Nehru was speaking, the Cold War was looming on the horizon. In Nehru's foreign policy, realpolitik, balance of power, and doctrinaire attitudes had no place whatsoever. His was a new and unsullied voice. He provided hope, if not diplomatic moksha.

A few days after the formation of the interim government, Nehru's mind turned to organizing the Asian Relations Conference. The conference was held in New Delhi from 23 March to 2 April 1947. Nothing practical came out of this get-together of a number of Asian countries, including Israel and Egypt. However, Nehru was more than satisfied. Actually he went over-board in calling the conference 'an amazing success from every point of view'. He added, 'I think we can definitely call it the beginning of a new era in Asian history.' There was no follow-up. No such second conference was organized by Nehru.

On 15 August 1947, independent India's tryst with destiny began. Jawaharlal Nehru had waited for 'The Appointed Day' all his adult life. Finally he was in the driver's seat and would remain there till his death.

Between 1947 and 1953, Nehru's international stature grew. Initially he got the worst of all worlds. Stalin's Russia and Mao's China looked on the Indian Prime Minister with disdain as the lackey of the imperialists and so on. But Nehru persevered. The turning point came during the Korean War in 1950–3. Nehru's views were taken seriously for the first time by Stalin and Mao. India not signing the Japanese Peace Treaty was welcomed by both. He became the natural leader of the Afro-Asian group of countries. He made non-alignment respectable. He was now looked upon as a sensitive and wise man who put principles above power politics. He was the statesman in the parleys of the Commonwealth. The international media fell for him. Even his verbal imprecision became diplomatic virtue.

I shall now briefly take up India's relations with the USA, USSR, China, and Pakistan and also Nehru's very specific contribution to international affairs and diplomacy.

USA

Sigmund Freud, the father of modern psychiatry once called the USA 'a gigantic mistake'. He could not have been more wrong.

The USA is the greatest success story in history. What is worrying is that from time to time the USA makes gigantic foreign policy mistakes. The most glaring examples are the non-recognition of Mao's China for twenty-two years and to go to war with Vietnam and invade Iraq.

Jawaharlal Nehru's intellectual centre of gravity was England. His first language was English. The books he read were written in English. He was not an original thinker but he was an outstanding communicator. His Western gurus were Bernard Shaw, Bertrand Russell, and Marx. History, not science or literature, was his passion. Two of his well-known books relate to history. In May 1922, he made a statement during his first trial which no other Indian of the time could have made.

> Less than ten years ago I returned from England after a lengthy stay there. I had passed through the usual course of public school and university. I had imbibed most of the prejudices of Harrow and Cambridge and in my likes and dislikes I was perhaps more an Englishman than an Indian. I looked upon the world almost from an Englishman's standpoint. And so I returned to India as much prejudiced in favour of England and the English as it was possible for an Indian to be.

It was hence not surprising that he looked at America through his English proclivities. He had read a fair amount of American history, was inspired by the Declaration of Independence and was an admirer of Abraham Lincoln and Franklin D. Roosevelt.

He had, nevertheless, been much irritated by the attitude of the USA in the Security Council debates on Kashmir. On 25 March 1948, in a letter to his ambassador in Washington, Vijayalakshmi Pandit, he wrote in exasperation, 'It is astonishing how naïve the Americans are in their foreign policy. It is only their money and their power that carries them through, not their intelligence or any other quality.'

Regardless, his first state visit was to the USA in October 1949. He spent over a month in the USA. The visit was not a memorable one. Nehru was sensitive to the attractive side of America but his meetings with President Harry Truman and his somewhat flamboyant Secretary of State, Dean Acheson were unsatisfactory. Acheson in his autobiography *Present at the Creation* wrote, '... he was one of the most difficult men with whom I have ever had to deal.'

While official America was disappointed with Nehru, the American press wrote about him in admiring terms. The *Christian Science Monitor* called him 'A World Titan'. Governor Adlai Stevenson of Illinois was even more effusive, 'Only a tiny handful of men have influenced the implacable forces of our time. To this small company of truly great, our guest belongs ... Pandit Jawaharlal Nehru belongs to the even smaller company of historic figures who wore a halo in their own lifetime!'

Nehru had, to some extent made America understand India and on his part he returned to India better informed. Yet there was no positive message from either side.

Bilateral relations started etiolating. The souring began soon after Nehru's return. Kashmir was the cause. The Americans were openly backing Pakistan. Nehru was also annoyed by the welcome soon given to Prime Minister Liaquat Ali Khan of Pakistan. As S. Gopal wrote, 'Nehru's vanity was hurt.'

Regardless, Nehru did not rush to the USSR. He disapproved that country's deterministic rigidity.

Truman was succeeded by Dwight D. Eisenhower as President in 1952. He selected John Foster Dulles as his Secretary of State. He was a man of vast experience, narrow outlook and carried his own China shop with him. The diplomatic crockery was flying all over the place. Nehru was faced with a peculiar situation. His advocacy of Mao's China entering the UN annoyed the Americans, without pleasing the Chinese.

The US and India had radically different approaches to world events. Nehru even went to the extent of noting that the fewer Indians went to America, the better.

Foster Dulles was rabidly anti-communist and established military pacts like Southeast Asia Treaty Organization (SEATO), Central Treaty Organization (CENTO) and Middle East Defence Organization (MEDO). Pakistan was the lynchpin of this anti-communist crusade. India was being cornered. The two countries drifted apart.

Diplomacy is a river that changes course when it comes to vital national interests. During the Suez crisis, India and the US found themselves on the same side of the table against Britain, France, and Israel. This coyness did not last long. The Americans began pumping military aid to Pakistan. Nehru was left with no choice but to turn to the USSR.

Dulles was briefly in New Delhi in 1956. He was careful in public and in his talks with Nehru he was far from abrasive. Nehru told the American that his support of Portugal on Goa was resented in India. Dulles said he had been guided by the advice of Indian experts in the State Department to which Nehru's response was that he was poorly advised.

Eisenhower was the first American President to come to India at the end of 1959. He was received with great warmth. At a rally at Ramlila Grounds, Delhi a crowd of a million people greeted Eisenhower. In his one to one talks with Indian leaders the President distanced himself from his Secretary of State. In his letter of 15 December 1959 to chief ministers, Nehru wrote, 'It may interest you to know that in the course of our talks, President Eisenhower told me that he appreciated and understands our desire to keep out of military alliances; indeed that he would not have it otherwise.'

This was welcome but on Kashmir, the American attitude did not alter, although Eisenhower did caution the Pakistanis that American arms supplied to them should not be used against India.

Another irritant in the Nehru administration was Krishna Menon. The US did not take to this moody, morbid, and disagreeable representative of

India. After meeting Menon in March and June 1955, Eisenhower described him as, 'a menace and a boor'. He was, to put it differently, the Indian John Foster Dulles.

Eisenhower and Nehru met for the last time at the UN in New York in 1960. It was the fifteenth anniversary of the founding of the UN. Eisenhower did not take kindly to Nehru not consulting him before tabling a resolution on behalf of Nasser, Tito, Soekarno, and Nkrumah, calling for a US-Soviet summit. Eisenhower rejected this suggestion and Nehru withdrew the resolution. Nehru spent four weeks in New York and returned disillusioned from the UN.

John F. Kennedy was sworn in as the thirty-fifth President of the USA. As a Senator he had sponsored the resolution asking for more economic aid for India. John Kennedy had his first meeting with Nehru in 1951 in New Delhi. The Indian prime minister did not show much interest in what the young Senator had to say. Regardless of this disappointment Kennedy considered Nehru as one of the eminent leaders of the world and praised his 'soaring idealism'.

Jawaharlal Nehru paid his last visit to Washington in November 1961, to meet and deliberate on world issues with Kennedy. Nehru was in one of his brooding and uncommunicative moods. In the words of B.K. Nehru, the Indian ambassador to the USA, Nehru's Washington stay was 'a disaster'. Kennedy was mystified by the remote silences of the prime minister. B.K. Nehru arranged a breakfast meeting with the best and brightest of the *New Frontier*. Here again the prime minister was not forthcoming. One of the guests in the meeting was Arthur Schlesinger, the eminent historian and author of *A Thousand Days*. He wrote in his book, 'I had the impression of an old man, his energies depleted, who heard things at a great distance and answered most questions with indifference.' President Kennedy described Nehru as the worst ever State visitor he had.

The Indian prime minister missed a great opportunity to establish even a working relationship with the American President. His inattention irritated the young Camelot team. In some mysterious way they felt let down.

A month later came the liberation of Goa. Kennedy was annoyed with Nehru for not taking him into confidence about Goa during their meeting a month before. At the UN, Ambassador Stevenson delivered one of his most sarcastic and anti-Krishna Menon tirades. Nehru made matters worse when in one of his letters to Kennedy he unnecessarily dragged in the name of 'the Cardinal Archbishop of Bombay, the highest dignitary of the Roman Catholic Church in India', who, he wrote, supported the Goa policy of Nehru. Kennedy, himself a Catholic, was not amused.

The reaction in the US to Indian action in Goa was one of unqualified indignation. I was at the time with the Permanent Mission of India at the UN and could not but notice how strong and widespread American reaction was. Kennedy himself said to B.K. Nehru,

> My only point is why you didn't do it before, 15 years before. But Mr. Ambassador, you spent the last 15 years preaching morality to us, and then you go ahead and act the way any normal country would behave and now that you have done what you should have done long ago, people are saying, the preacher has been caught coming out of the brothel. And they are clapping. And Mr. Ambassador, I want to tell you, I am clapping too.

The Americans over-reacted. The President's displeasure was short-lived. He went out of his way to give all possible assistance to Nehru when China attacked India in October 1962. Kennedy's hands were full with the Cuban missile crisis, yet he responded to Nehru's desperate pleading. Ironically, Kennedy was assassinated six months before Jawaharlal Nehru's death on 27 May 1964.

The Indo-US relations during the Nehru era could be summed up by citing the titles of two novels by Charles Dickens—*Great Expectations* and *Hard Times*.

USSR

As has already been mentioned, the youthful Jawaharlal Nehru was intellectually much affected by the Soviet State he first encountered in 1927. The 1917 Russian Revolution in many ways altered the international power equations. Being the great man that he was, he, after 1947, did not jump into the Soviet lap. The Indian communists had almost declared war on Nehru's newly formed government and they were being encouraged and supported by Stalin.

If that was not enough, Stalin considered India a client state of the Anglo-Americans and India's membership of the Commonwealth was, according to the Soviet leaders, another example of Nehru's subservience.

Nehru, a lover of words and phrases used restraint when it came to the written word. Yet the Russian attitude so exasperated him that on 26 June 1948, he wrote to Krishna Menon:

> We want friendship and cooperation with Russia in many fields but we are a sensitive people and we react strongly to being cursed at and run down. The whole basis of Russian policy appears to be that no essential change has taken place in India and that we still continue to be camp followers of the British. That, of course, is complete nonsense and if a policy is based on nonsensical premises it is apt to go wrong.

Nehru sent his sister Vijayalakshmi Pandit as ambassador to the Soviet Union. She stayed there till 1949. Stalin did not receive her.

Dr S. Radhakrishnan, who succeeded her, was an inspired choice. He was an internationally respected man of letters, a link between the past and present of India, deeply religious yet modern, and an eloquent and nationalist humanist. He had a very British sense of humour. He landed at Moscow airport with *The God that Failed*, a collection of essays by six former Communists such as Arthur Koestler, Stephen Spender, Ignazio Silone, and Louis Fischer.

This was Radhakrishnan's first exposure to the Soviet Union. He had been invited twice, once in 1927 and again in 1943, but could not get away from India for reasons beyond his control. He read systematically a number of books on conditions in the USSR. He was acquainted with the writings of Marx and Lenin. He told the Soviets that India followed an independent foreign policy and India's 'connections with the Western powers had not diminished her independence'.

Stalin was 'intrigued' by Radhakrishnan. S. Gopal, in his masterly biography of his father has written a captivating account of the unconventional Indian representative in Stalin's Moscow. Stalin observed, 'I would like to meet the ambassador who spends his time in bed—writing.' Stalin's Russia was for diplomats a comfortable prison. Radhakrishnan took a long-term view of Indo-Soviet relations. He explained to the Soviets what nonalignment was all about. After their meeting, Stalin's interpreter told Radhakrishnan that Stalin liked his frankness and that he was not 'an ordinary ambassador'.

So long as Stalin was alive, no positive diplomatic move from the USSR was initiated. Stalin died on 5 March 1953. It took his successors—

Malenkov, Khrushchev, Bulganin, and others—some time to settle down. By the end of 1954, Indo-Soviet relations had taken an upward turn. The coming months witnessed unusual mutual warmth. The climax came when Nehru paid an official visit to the USSR.

Jawaharlal Nehru arrived in Moscow on 7 June 1955 for an extended stay. He received an exceptionally warm and friendly reception. His discussions with V.M. Molotov, Nikolai Bulganin, Voroshilov, Nikita Khrushchev and others were devoted more to international affairs rather than bilateral relations.

The most significant discussion was on the forthcoming Big Four meeting in Geneva. Jawaharlal Nehru made the observation that China, India, and other South East Asian countries representing one billion people would not be represented at the conference.

In the USSR he specifically mentioned that the meeting of the Atomic Energy Conference to be held in Geneva under the Chairmanship of H.C. Bhabha would 'be incomplete without China'.

Nehru addressed a public meeting at the Dynamo stadium in Moscow on 21 June 1955.

In his speech, he spoke about Gandhi and India's belief in peaceful co-existence. But China was given special treatment. 'It is in recognition of the right of each country to fashion its own destiny that the Government of India and the People's Government of China agreed to Five Principles to govern their relations with each other ... We have long felt that the non-recognition by the UN of the great People's Republic of China is ... an anomaly ...'

In Nehru's deliberations with Prime Minister Nikolai Bulganin, an extraordinary proposal was made by the Soviet leader. He said, '... while we are discussing the general international situation and reducing tension, we propose suggesting at a later stage India's inclusion as the sixth (permanent) member of the Security Council.'

Nehru responded in Olympian language,

Perhaps Mr. Bulganin knows that some people in the USA have suggested that India should replace China in the Security Council. This is to create trouble between us and China. We are, of course, wholly opposed to it. Further, we are opposed to pushing ourselves forward to occupy certain positions because that may itself create difficulties and might itself become a subject of controversy. If

India is to be admitted to the Security Council it raises the question of the revision of the charter of the U.N. We feel this should not be done till the question of China's admission is first solved.

Bulganin accepted Nehru's argument.

Nehru could not but be affected by the welcome he received. It was not simply a tribute to an individual but to his country and the realization by the Soviet leaders that India mattered and it was following an independent non-aligned foreign policy.

In December the same year, Khrushchev and Bulganin visited India. The record of the discussion between Nehru and the ebullient Khrushchev gives the texture of the talks. Nehru was urbane, Oxbridge, and restrained while Khrushchev was crude, forthright, uninhibited, a working class man coming from a poor family, seasoned by war, and was unbridled in his criticism of the USA and the UK and the deplorable colonial record of European powers. Nehru was uncomfortable with the verbal excesses of Khrushchev and in his letter to the chief ministers dwelt on this at some length. The USA and UK took strong exception to Khrushchev's outbursts in India.

On most international matters there were broad similarities of views. The unequivocal support of Khrushchev to India on Kashmir and Goa was most appreciated. The Soviet leaders joined Nehru in criticizing the creation of the Baghdad Pact.

About the activities of the Communist Party of India, Nehru left his guests in no doubt about his total disapproval of these.

> I said that the Communist Party of India was not strong and its leaders not very intelligent. We were not worried by their activities here, but what worried me was the effect of those on Indo-Soviet relations. It was widely believed that the Communist Party here and elsewhere received their directions from Moscow. Indeed the behaviour of the Communist Party leaders in India supported this. They rushed to Moscow repeatedly for directions and came back and said, on the authority of Moscow, what should be done. They appeared to be supplied with large funds, although their sources of income in India were limited...

Khrushchev expressed surprise and feigned ignorance.

The biggest meeting in the tour was held in Calcutta (now Kolkata) to welcome the Soviet leaders; two million people filled the Maidan. This gave the Russians a dramatic picture of Indian democracy and the popularity of Nehru.

The visit brought India and the USSR much closer. But such is the speed and unpredictability of international affairs that in less than a year a shadow was cast. The Soviet intervention in Hungary in late 1956 caught Nehru off guard. Krishna Menon, disregarding Nehru's instructions on a Security Council Resolution made matters worse. Nehru was quick enough to observe the widespread and vocal denunciation of his equivocal stand on Soviet military action against a popular revolt in Hungary. It was an appalling diplomatic misjudgement. He made amends but his initial reaction succeeded in dissatisfying both the North Atlantic Treaty Organization (NATO) countries and the Soviets.

It is, however, no exaggeration to say that the Soviet Union helped Nehru to safeguard India's independence and sovereignty. The real test came in 1962, when the Soviet Union decided on pro-Indian neutrality which caused much anger in Peking.

Kashmir

'For me Kashmir's future is of the most intimate personal significance'
—Jawaharlal Nehru to Sheikh Abdullah, 10 October 1947

The literature on the Kashmir issue is vast. The contribution in this case is by none other than Jawaharlal Nehru. It goes against my grain to question the judgement of so great a man. The melancholy fact is that Nehru converted an entirely domestic matter into an international one. This was no ordinary blunder. Some writers have blamed Sardar Patel for not taking enough interest in Jammu and Kashmir, because he was busy integrating over 500 princely states into the Dominion of India. Without the Sardar's dedication to this cause, we would have had several more Kashmirs. Nevertheless, he had not washed his hands off Kashmir. Patel was a realist and farsighted statesman, action-oriented, not given to vaporous pronouncements. Even before the Maharajas acceded to India on 27 October 1947, Sardar Patel wrote to the Defence Minister, Sardar Baldev Singh on 7 October 1947, 'I hope arrangements are in train to send immediately supplies of arms and ammunition to Kashmir state. If necessary we must arrange to send them by air ... I think the question of military assistance in time of emergency must claim the attention of our Defence Council as soon as possible ...'

Before I deal with the events of the fateful week—22–27 October 1947, let me state that Sardar Patel's instructions were scuttled by the British Commander-in-Chief (of India) in consultation with the Supreme Commander-in-Chief of India and Pakistan without the knowledge of the Indian government.

The Kashmiri government was desperately asking India for arms; nothing was done till 22 October when Pakistan launched the invasion of the Jhelum valley. India learnt of this on 24 October. Nehru spoke to Mountbatten. Kashmir was now becoming an Indian problem. But Mountbatten, and the three armed services chiefs—all Englishmen—in both countries had their own agenda. The British chiefs of the two states were in daily touch with each other and secretly informing India's Governor General of day to day events. Mountbatten kept Nehru in the dark. Not only that, he used the British High Commission in New Delhi to send messages to Prime Minister Attlee and the King—all behind the back of a government of which he was Governor General.

On looking back, one is confounded by the fact that the last Viceroy of India was invited by Nehru to become the first Governor General of India. This should never have been done. Jinnah was wiser. When Mountbatten suggested that he be the Governor General of Pakistan also; Jinnah turned him down.

Over the years, my assessment of Mountbatten has been revised. Personally we got on well but his Indian record has to be demythologized. Mountbatten was a hustler. He had himself nominated as Chairman of the joint Defence Committee. This should never have been agreed to by Nehru.

On 25 October 1947, the grave situation in Kashmir was not taken up by the cabinet but by the Defence Committee with Mountbatten in the chair. C. Dasgupta in his revealing book *War and Diplomacy in Kashmir, 1947–48* has this to say about the overbearing, charming, and meddling Governor General of India.

It permitted Mountbatten, as Chairman of the Defence Committee, to play a critical role in policy making, a role from which he would have been excluded if the initial deliberations had taken place in a meeting of the full cabinet. Moreover, the meeting on 25 October established a precedent till the end of 1947; all important questions relating to Kashmir were decided not in the Cabinet but in the meetings of the Defence Committee. This allowed Mountbatten to play a role which far exceeded that of a constitutional figurehead and which culminated, at the end of the year, in the decision to refer the Kashmir issue to the United Nations.

The Commander-in-Chief of the Indian army, General Rob Lockhart, in a meeting had the temerity to ask Nehru and Patel whether Kashmir was of vital importance to India. The prime minister, instead of pulling up Lockhart for his impertinence, said that Kashmir was vital for India's secularism.

Mountbatten's intention was to prevent Indian troops being sent to Srinagar before the Maharaja acceded to India. Regardless, troops were flown to Srinagar on 27 October, arriving just in time to prevent Srinagar falling into the hands of the Pakistanis. The Maharaja signed the instrument of accession the same day.

It is, even after sixty-three years, a strain to condone Nehru for accepting Mountbatten's advice to take the issue to the United Nations.

A draft was prepared for a communication to the UN Security Council. Mountbatten was in favour of the Indian draft being shown to Liaquat Ali Khan, but Nehru refused.

Patel was not in favour of even a limited reference to the United Nations (he called it the Disunited Nations). Nehru had the wisdom to show the draft to Gandhiji who made a vital correction to cut out, in pencil, the words, 'independent status'. S. Gopal refers to this in Volume Two of his biography of Nehru.

It is now well-known that Nehru later deeply regretted his accepting Mountbatten's advice to take the Kashmir issue to the UN. But the deed was done in a manner which even today appals me. S. Gopal concedes that 'by reference to the Security Council, India stood to suffer in every way'.

India sent her complaint to the United Nations Security Council under Chapter VI of the UN Charter, which is exclusively for 'Pacific Settlement of Disputes'.

Thus, India, *ab initio* accepted that a dispute existed. Who suggested this to the prime minister is not important. That such a decision was taken with the full approval of the prime minister is of importance. What were the members of the Security Council expected to do when India herself accepted that Kashmir was disputed territory?

Was an alternative available? Yes. We should have appealed to the Security Council, under chapter VII of the UN Charter. That chapter refers to 'Action with Respect to Threats to the Peace, and Acts of Aggression'.

The consequences of this inadequately thought through decision distorted Nehru's foreign policy and made India hostage to the Security Council. The assumption that India would be fairly and justly treated was confusing hope with reality. This was an example of political innocence in a state of rare purity.

At a meeting called by Mountbatten on 25 February 1948, Nehru said 'that it had been an act of faith by the government of India, at a time when the situation was rapidly deteriorating, to make their reference to the Security Council in the first place. If this faith was now proved to be misplaced, the consequences would have to be borne by those who had made the reference.'

Sardar Patel was also present at this meeting. He did not mince words. He said, 'Nehru in particular had great faith in the institution of UNO. But the Security Council had been meddling in power politics to such an extent that very little of this faith was left.' He pointed out that it had been the Governor General who had induced the Government to make the reference to the UN in the first place. With this the Governor General agreed.

Pakistan could have wished for nothing more suitable. It has kept Kashmir on the international agenda for sixty-three years and has bedevilled Indo-Pak relations ever since. Indian diplomats spent 25 per cent of their time on defending India's case throughout the world for almost three decades.

Our very first delegation to the Security Council included Sheikh Abdullah. He was no pushover. Even in 1948, he had an independent Kashmir at the back of his mind. Howard B. Schaffer in his book on Kashmir writes, 'The Indians had made Abdullah a member of their UN delegation, no doubt in the expectation that he would be an effective spokesman for India's cause. They could not have calculated that he would undercut their position by calling for Kashmir's independence in a private conversation with Austin who was the US delegate in the Security Council.'

Jawaharlal Nehru had put all his Kashmiri eggs in the Abdullah basket. Gradually Sheikh Abdullah started distancing himself from Nehru and

India. By 1952, he was openly speaking of an independent Kashmir. Events took an unexpected turn and the charismatic Sheikh was arrested on 8 August 1953.

Nehru devoted much of his time and energy to Kashmir. In 1957 Krishna Menon addressed the Security Council for nine hours. He became a quasi-hero in India but made little impact in the Council. Some of the members friendly to India commented, 'If you have such a good case then why a nine-hour speech?' Most Security Council delegates descended into a semi-somnolent state. Diplomats normally do not act thus. But Krishna Menon had tried their patience.

I am not putting down what transpired on Kashmir between 1957 and 1964; it is too well-known. After the Sino-Indian war, some bizarre events of momentous concern unfolded. A dejected and demoralized Nehru was pressurized by the USA, UK, and Mountbatten. Nehru was told that he alone could settle with Pakistan on Kashmir. In November, A. Harriman and Duncan Sandys arrived in New Delhi to pressurize Nehru. It was a dismal situation. A very sick Prime Minister was being asked to solve the Kashmir issue to the advantage of Pakistan. A sarcastic account of these melancholy events is given by Y.D. Gundevia, in his entertaining book *Outside the Archives*. He was at the time Commonwealth Secretary in the External Affairs Ministry. Gundevia has also deftly caricatured Mountbatten, who was an active meddler.

It was only after Nehru's death in May 1964, that new thinking on Kashmir became possible. Sardar Swaran Singh, a Sikh Jat, was appointed External Affairs Minister by Prime Minister Lal Bahadur Shastri. Once again the Indo-Pak-Kashmir question was taken to the Security Council by Pakistan in September 1965. Sardar Swaran Singh arrived in New York for the meeting. Z.A. Bhutto too made his appearance. The contrast between the earthy, slow-moving Sikh Jat and the cigar-smoking, whisky-drinking, and sartorially elegant Bhutto with a commitment to philandering, was all too evident. It was simplicity versus sophistication; tortoise versus hare. The former won.

On the advice of Ambassador Parathasarthi, Narendra Singh, Brajesh Mishra, and myself the External Affairs Minister, after some reluctance agreed to walk out of the council, if Bhutto used unbridled and abusive language. Bhutto obliged. The entire Indian delegation walked out. The

Pakistani delegation and the Security Council were stunned. The secret of the walkout was not known to anyone except the five Indians. Consequently no photographers were present to record this unprecedented step of the Indian delegation. It did the trick. Kashmir was never again taken up by the Security Council. The walkout had the approval of Prime Minister Lal Bahadur Shastri.

Bilaterally, the issue continues to sour India-Pakistan relations to this day. What cannot be cured must be endured.

Non-alignment

Even before 1947, Nehru had, in his writings and speeches emphasized that an independent India would follow an independent policy. It would keep away from power politics.

Non-alignment to Nehru was not a dogma or a doctrine. It was a state of mind. It was an instrument for strengthening the forces of peace, disarmament, and economic cooperation and to provide a platform for the newly independent countries of Asia, Africa, and South America. Non-alignment was not neutrality. Nehru did not subscribe to the assumptions of the Cold War. He refused to have anything to do with them, maintaining a deliberate distance from its proponents. For those who looked at diplomacy and foreign policy in black and white terms, he had little patience. He pointed out that in between black and white there was a large grey area. India was non-aligned *ab initio*.

The hard core of Non-alignment meant retaining 'our thought, judgement and action under conditions of the Cold War'. Nehru was neither apologetic nor aggressive about Non-alignment. Wherever he travelled he spoke of its relevance. His nuanced approach made a subtle difference between Non-alignment and a Non-aligned Movement (NAM). Krishna Menon succeeded in convincing Nehru that the formation of NAM was inevitable and unavoidable. This finally occurred in 1961 in Belgrade where the first Summit meeting of NAM was held. It was the only NAM Summit Nehru partook in.

Nehru, no doubt was allergic to neutrality and passivity. 'We have sought to avoid foreign entanglements by not joining one bloc or another. Inevitably it means we have sought to plough a lonely furrow. Nonetheless, that is the only honourable and right position to take and I am quite sure that by adopting that position, we shall ultimately gain in national and international prestige.'

The NAM was growing in numbers. The West began to take NAM seriously when they saw Nehru, Nasser, Tito, Soekarno, and Nkrumah as its leading lights. Non-alignment was badly bruised and battered in 1962 when China invaded India. It was not the NAM that came to Nehru's aid but the US and UK. Nehru himself accepted, 'We have been living in a make-belief world.'

I continue to share Nehru's vision of Non-alignment. It is obvious that the NAM has to be reinvented to address and find answers to the problems that confront humanity today. The current menaces are terrorism, globalization, environment, climate change, drug trafficking, galloping income disparities, HIV, AIDs and last but not the least, Islamic fundamentalism. Regrettably, India has not taken the initiative to change and reform NAM. Actually we have shown little interest in this process, except paying lip service.

Is non-alignment relevant, now that the Cold War is over, the Soviet bloc is history, the world has run out of colonies, etc.? In answer to that one asks (and Nehru would have posed the same question), how is NATO relevant? The Cold War is over, the Soviet bloc is history, the world has run out of colonies, yet NATO has expanded to the borders of Russia. Where is the enemy?

No government in India has jettisoned non-alignment. None can. The alternative is to bow to the US, and that the Indian people will never endorse.

Finally, to every NAM Summit, the USA, China, Russia, UK, France, Canada, and Japan send very senior observers. Why? Simply, because so large an organization as NAM cannot be ignored.

China

Jawaharlal Nehru believed that the People's Republic of China and the Republic of India could not only coexist but should have the closest and friendliest relations. He bent backwards to accommodate Mao's China. His thinking was that harmonious relations between the two oldest Asian civilizations, the two largest Asian countries were to be welcomed not only bilaterally, but these were important also for Asia and the world. Nehru had a somewhat romantic view of China—the pre-Mao China.

Jawaharlal Nehru often said that the two countries had not gone to war for 2000 years. How could they have? The human traffic for over a thousand years was minimal. Buddhists monks, with superhuman effort did come and go, but their numbers were insignificant. Travel facilities were nonexistent. Hence, the talk about no war in two millennia was somewhat misplaced. S. Gopal, a Nehruite like me, concedes that 'Nehru's assessment of China's attitude to India was naïve'. Nehru was familiar with the history of the pre-Mao Tse Tung China. But he certainly misread the thinking, motives, and long-term objectives of Mao's China. When one comes to think of it, the Sino-Indian honeymoon was short-lived (1954–8).

The early warnings were ignored by Nehru. Sardar Patel was far less credulous. In a letter to Nehru, dated 7 November 1950, Patel dealt at length with Nehru's Tibet-China policy.

> I have carefully gone through the correspondence between the External Affairs Ministry and our Ambassador in Peking and through him the Chinese Government. I have tried to peruse this correspondence as favourably to our Ambassador and the Chinese Government as possible, but I regret to say that neither of them comes out well as a result of this study. The Chinese Government has tried to delude us by professions of peaceful intentions. My own feeling is that at a crucial period they managed to instil into our Ambassador a false sense of confidence in their so-called desire to settle the Tibetan problem by peaceful means ... Our Ambassador has been at great pains to find an explanation or justification for Chinese policy and actions ...

At the end of his letter Sardar Patel has made a number of suggestions to Nehru. One of these was 'a military and intelligence appreciation of the Chinese threat to India both on the frontier and to internal security'.

Even a cool-headed Secretary General of the Ministry of External Affairs, Sir Girija Shankar Bajpai sent notes to the prime minister on 27 and 31 October 1950. He wrote,

> What interest the Ambassador thinks he may be serving by showing so much solicitude for the Chinese Government's policy of false excuses and wanton high-handedness towards Tibet passes my understanding ... I feel it my duty to observe that, in handling the Tibetan issue with the Chinese Government, our Ambassador has allowed himself to be influenced more by the Chinese point of view, by Chinese claims, by Chinese maps and by regard for Chinese susceptibilities than by his instructions or by India's interests.

S. Gopal gently writes about 'the shortcomings of our diplomacy in Peking'. Panikkar had converted the word 'suzerainty' to 'sovereignty' on his own with regard to Tibet. This must have been music to Chinese ears.

What did Jawaharlal Nehru think of K.M. Panikkar? On 14 September 1950, he wrote to his sister, who was an Ambassador to the USA, 'Panikkar has done a good job and gets on well with the Chinese Government. I have no doubt that the friendly influence we have exercised on China during the past few months has helped the cause of peace...'

Thus there was a serious disconnect on a vital issue between the Prime Minister and Sardar Patel. Jawaharlal Nehru did not reply to Patel's letter, but in notes to the Secretary General, he indirectly disagreed with Patel's approach. He wrote, '... I rule out any major attack on India by China. I think these considerations should be borne in mind, because there is far too much loose talk about China attacking and overrunning India.'

Sardar Vallabhbhai Patel passed away on 15 December 1950.

However, negotiations between India and the Peoples' Republic of China on the relations between India and Tibet opened in Peking on 31 December 1953 and concluded on 29 April 1954. The full title of the Agreement was a mouthful—Agreement Between India and China on Trade and Intercourse between India and Tibet Region of China.

The preamble to the Agreement was of vital importance as it gave birth to Panchsheel. Jawaharlal Nehru elaborated on the Agreement and the potent Preamble in the Lok Sabha on 15 May 1954.

> A very important event to which I would like to draw the attention of the House is the Agreement between India and China in regard to Tibet. The agreement deals with a large number of problems, each one of them not very important in itself perhaps, but important from the point of view of our trade, our pilgrim traffic, our trade posts, our communications there and the rest ... The major thing about this Agreement is the Preamble to the Agreement.

It is necessary to quote the preamble in full:

> The Principles and considerations which govern our mutual relations and the approach of the two countries to each other are as follows:
> (1) Mutual respect for each other's territorial integrity and sovereignty; (2) Mutual non-aggression; (3) Mutual non-interference in each other's internal affairs; (4) Equality and mutual benefit; and (5) Peaceful coexistence.

The prose is neither elegant nor uplifting.

What was not made public was that the agreement also would promote trade and cultural intercourse between the Tibet region of China and India. The Agreement also provided for establishment of trade agencies by China and India and visits by traders and pilgrims of both countries. It also provided for the lapse of certain rights and privileges previously exercised in Tibet by the Government of India.

In the notes appended to the Agreement it was agreed that the government of India would withdraw within six months the military escort stationed at Yatung and Gyantse in Tibet.

India was not invited to the Indo-China Conference held in Geneva in 1954. Nevertheless, Nehru sent Krishna Menon to be an observer. In the course of three weeks Krishna Menon had 200 interviews. Chou En Lai was leading the Chinese delegation. Krishna Menon attracted his attention. He found Menon intelligent and helpful. Krishna Menon, like so many others, was bowled over by the Chinese Prime Minister. He wrote to Nehru from Geneva, 'Chou is a fine man and I believe that the Chinese have no expansionist ideas ... I found little difficulty in getting near him ... He is extremely shrewd and observant, very Chinese but modern.'

On his return journey to China, Chou stopped in New Delhi. The two—Nehru and Chou—met for the first time; both of them were urbane, sophisticated, charismatic, and good-looking.

Chou En Lai, an accomplished actor, played his unctuous role to perfection. He used silken smooth flattery, 'Your Excellency has more knowledge about the world and Asia than I have. I am not being modest. Your Excellency has participated much more in international affairs than I have. We have been shut up in our own country dealing with our own human problems.'

Jawaharlal Nehru was human and rather relished the praise Chou heaped on him. Chou had briefly mentioned the border. Nehru with Chou's consent omitted a reference to the border in the communiqué. This was not a negligible error.

Jawaharlal Nehru visited China in October 1954. He received a tremendous popular welcome. No one in our embassy informed him that such welcomes were far from spontaneous. These were state-sponsored.

In spite of the welcome and warmth in Sino-Indian relations, Nehru did raise the issue of India's borders and the inaccuracy in Chinese maps.

Chou's reply was the usual one That the Kuomintang maps had not been revised because the People's Government had had no time to revise them. Nehru was satisfied and this map question caused him no concern because according to him India's boundary was well defined and it was not a subject for discussion. Here again he took too much for granted. He should, at some stage, have insisted that China accept India's position in writing.

Nehru's conversations with Mao Tse Tung were cordial but conjunction of minds was missing. Mao's views on the aftermath of nuclear war shocked Nehru. With Chou En Lai, Nehru had agreeable and wide-ranging discussions. The Chinese Prime Minister sought Nehru's help for China being invited to the Bandung conference in April 1955. This Nehru ensured.

It was at Bandung that Chou really arrived on the international stage. He performed brilliantly and met the leader of every delegation. His speech too was carefully prepared. Jawaharlal Nehru, in real friendship, took Chou under his wing. Publicly, the Chinese Prime Minister was appreciative, but privately he made it known that Nehru was patronizing.

It could not escape the Mao government that in 1955, Nehru's worldwide prestige was at its peak. He seemed unassailable. Even the erstwhile critics conceded that Nehru was a world figure. He may not have been seen as the saviour of the world but he came very near it in public perception.

The Chinese were fully aware of Nehru getting closer to the Soviets. They also watched with concern his rapport with Eisenhower.

Differences were privately expressed by Nehru about Soviet intervention in Hungary in the autumn of 1956 when Chou En Lai who had been to Moscow and to East European countries, came to India immediately thereafter. Nehru and he agreed to differ on Hungary—Chou toeing the Soviet line.

Unknown to us the Chinese built a road in Aksai Chin in 1958. This was a violation of our sovereignty. Our reconnaissance party discovered it much later. Nehru still hoped that this particular incident should not derail Sino-Indian relations and said nothing in public because he still believed that Chou En Lai had in 1956 accepted the Indian alignment. As late as December 1957 Nehru made a statement in Parliament that there was not the remotest chance of a military conflict with China. He was more worried about 'the Naga trouble from this point of view than about any [thing] that the Chinese may do'. By 1958, China's intentions became clear. They claimed 40,000 square miles of Indian territory. The maps were not corrected.

Then came the flight of the Dalai Lama to India in March 1959. India, keeping with its age-old tradition granted asylum to the Buddhist leader. From then on it was downhill all the way. China forgot Panchsheel and Nehru was virulently criticized in the Chinese press. The Dalai Lama's activities were distorted and condemned. The border became an area of conflict and the hopes of Nehru received a nasty jolt. A final attempt was made to resolve Sino-India differences in April 1960.

Chou En Lai and his Foreign Minister Chen Yi arrived in New Delhi to find a solution. I have written about this fateful visit in my book *My China Diary*. The gulf between India and China by now was so wide that after six days of intense negotiations no common ground was found. War came in October 1962. We were beaten. China had made its point. Their troops withdrew behind the McMahon Line and declared a unilateral ceasefire.

Nehru's belief that a war between China and India could lead to a World War proved totally misplaced. In the same month of October, the world was busy with the Cuban missile crisis. At one time it looked as if a nuclear war would break out.

Yet Kennedy promptly came to Nehru's rescue. We all remember Nixon sending the 7th US fleet to the Bay of Bengal in 1971. It is never recalled that Kennedy too sent the air craft carrier Enterprise to the Bay in 1962. This was also Kennedy's signal to China, thus far and no further. The US had never made any pretence about its worldwide strategic network and involvement. Had Sardar Patel's suggestions made in his letter to Nehru in November 1950 been acted upon, we might have fared better in 1962. Nehru's excessive faith in Krishna Menon added to the Prime Minister's headaches. He, finally, but reluctantly had to get rid of him. Nehru failed to understand the mind and method of Mao Tse Tung, who, besides being a nationalist, was also a 'skilled practioner of *real politik*'. For this Nehruvian lapse, India paid dearly. Nehru's prestige plummeted. He was never the same man again. He, mercifully for himself, passed away on 27 May 1964.

He was a remarkable Prime Minister. He was a statesman of high standing. He was a humanist. Was he a great foreign minister? The jury is still out.

M.V. KAMATH

9

Jawaharlal Nehru as I Saw Him

My memories of the Nehru family go back to the 1930s when Motilal Nehru passed away. I was born and brought up in a small town called Udupi which was a Congress stronghold. The people decided that the passing away of Motilalji should be observed suitably and a decision was made to take out a procession to be led by an elephant on the back of which one was to be seated holding a large portrait of Motilalji for all to see. I was chosen for the job. I was hardly eleven years old and riding an elephant holding a portrait was a frightening experience. I had never ridden on an elephant before and I had to be held firmly by the waist by the mahout who was sitting behind me to see that I did not fall. Many watched the lengthy procession from both sides of the road and respectfully paid their homage to the portrait. Till Motilalji was alive, Jawaharlal, his son, largely remained in the background, even if he had presided over the Lahore session of the Indian National Congress in December 1929, at which a demand was made for 'complete independence'.

Then came 1936, which saw the release of Jawaharlal's autobiography. My father had bought a copy which I read avidly. I was then all of fifteen but by then Jawaharlal had become a hero for me, as for my generation. He had one long spell in the gaol—one of his longest, a total of 1170 days—between December 1931 and September 1935. It was an impressive sacrifice to make which commanded our respect. It was during the time he spent in jail that he had written his memoirs and it came as a revelation. We got to know a great deal more about our icon. I was greatly impressed by the fact that he had been tutored by an Englishman before he was sent to England to study in a famous English school and later at the University of Cambridge. Brought up though as I was in an average middle-class family, I was not envious. I was impressed. His autobiography, if I remember all right, was dedicated to his wife: 'Kamala who is no more'. That added to my respect for Jawaharlal.

At fifteen, I was like all my contemporaries, deeply interested in the freedom movement. Jawaharlal was elected as Congress president in 1936, and the news was received with enthusiasm. I wore khadi; I spun on the charkha. I read the then available journals and newspapers, importantly *The Hindu* from Madras, the Sunday edition of *Bombay Chronicle* and another Madras-based Sunday weekly called *The Sunday Times* for news about the national movement, and the freedom struggle as such. But by then another congress leader, Subhas Chandra Bose, was catching my teenage imagination. It was a struggle to choose between Jawaharlal and Subhas Chandra Bose. Often it was Bose who was more captivating. There was something exciting about Bose that could not be ignored.

It was only when I came to Bombay (now Mumbai) in May 1939, that for the first time I became fully engaged in reading up on Congress politics. I had joined St Xavier's College in June 1939, to do my B.Sc. In September, the Second World War broke out and then, it seemed, all hell broke as well. Congress parties in power in various provinces resigned and now I could see events at close quarters. To be then in Bombay felt like heaven. Congress leaders came frequently to the city to address public meetings which I regularly attended since I had become a Congress volunteer. In 1939, I was all of eighteen and had come of age.

I read nationalist newspapers like the *Bombay Chronicle* and *The Free Press Journal* and followed Congress politics with keen interest. I heard

Subhas Chandra Bose—for the first and last time, I am afraid—when he addressed a meeting in Bombay; he had practically broken up with the Congress and separated from colleagues like Jawaharlal. His subsequent house arrest, the way he escaped to go all the way from Calcutta (now Kolkata) to Kabul and then in turn to Moscow, Rome, Berlin, and finally Tokyo made him a legend. My admiration for Jawaharlal did not diminish but my admiration for Bose increased by leaps and bounds.

I graduated in 1941, but remained a Congress volunteer and was present at the 7–9 August 1942 Congress meeting at Gowalia Tank when it passed the Quit India resolution. Following the wholesale arrest of the Congress leaders on 10 August there were large meetings of protest at which I was also present, watching how people were being lathi-charged. Then followed an interregnum, when all seemed quiet. The war was slowly coming to an end with the Allies assured of victory. Jawaharlal was released in June 1945, just before the Simla Conference was convened by the Viceroy, Lord Wavell. And Subhas Chandra Bose was reported killed in an air crash. That took away the only competitor to Nehru for my fulsome admiration. Once more it was to Nehru that one looked up to, even more so than to Mahatma Gandhi. In 1940, the Congress had declined to accept non-violence as a shield against external danger. In 1946–7 the Congress again refused to embrace it against internal disorder. It was not that I admired Gandhiji less, only I admired Nehru more.

I literally grew up as Nehru's popularity was in ascendance. The Lahore Congress had brought Jawaharlal to the forefront of national politics, but it was not until the late 1930s, as B.R. Nanda has written, that Panditji had become a factor to be reckoned with in the higher echelons of the Congress. He was the only Congress leader who made an all-India tour, prior to 1937, to plead for Congress success in the elections to follow. It was a fantastic effort which brought encomia to Jawaharlal as an indefatigable leader. He has had differences with his colleagues but Gandhiji had stood by him. In October 1945, a few months before the negotiations for the final demission of British power began, Gandhiji had written to Jawaharlal: 'I am an old man ... I have therefore named you as my heir.' It was Jawaharlal that he preferred as his successor when he could well have nominated Sardar Vallabhbhai Patel, the so-called Strong Man in the party.

In early 1946, I joined *The Free Press Journal* of Bombay as a reporter and now I had a greater chance to see Jawaharlal professionally. A government had yet to be formed in Delhi and Jawaharlal was still politically just a leader, not a Prime Minister. It so happened that he had an occasion to visit Bombay. Those were the days when there were no air flights and rich or poor, citizens had to move around in trains. Jawaharlal's visit from Delhi to Bombay had been announced with the date and time of his arrival and the train he was to take. I knew that once he arrived in Bombay he would not give me—a rookie—an opportunity to interview him. I, therefore, worked out a daring plan to interview him through whatever means. In those days Jawaharlal travelled without security. The Railway authorities, aware of his status, would provide him with a small bogie in which he was to be the sole occupant. No one else was allowed to enter it and nobody would have dared to, anyway. I, along with a colleague named Venkateswaran from *The Indian Express* and my photographer Gilbert Austin decided to do the unbelievable. We knew the train would stop for half an hour at Kalyan. So the three of us went to Kalyan an hour before the expected time of arrival of the train and found out from the Station Master where the Nehru bogie was expected to be when the train halted. When finally the train arrived, we went over to the other side of the train and sneaked into Nehru's bogie. We were lucky. The door had not been closed.

Two things were in our favour. One was that we could get in without being noticed. The other was that Jawaharlal was engaged in waving to the crowds which had gathered on the platform, vigorously shouting: 'Jawaharlal Nehru ki jai!' He had not noticed that the three of us had entered his cabin like a bunch of thieves, without prior permission.

A few minutes later the train began to move, and it was then that he saw us. To this day I am surprised why he did not pull the chain, stop the train and get us thrown out, if not arrested. He just got back to his seat and started reading a book ignoring all three of us totally.

He had in front of him a stack of books and I noticed that the topmost book had the title: *The Green Hat*. The name of the author was Michael Arlen. Delighted that I could write a story about this, I took out my notebook and began scribbling, when noticing me he asked: 'Who are you?' All three of us, to be honest, were behaving like frightened chicks. We had broken the law and could be punished. But Jawaharlal did not sound offended, so I told him that all three of us were from the media, I was from *The Free Press Journal* and Venky was from the *Express*. Austin with his camera did not have to be introduced.

The train came to a halt much behind Thane station. We could see beyond the window a highway choked with trucks loaded with war material, all of which had become redundant, the war being over. Suddenly Jawaharlal came to life. 'Look at that!' he said, pointing to the trucks, 'Such a waste of public money. What are you gentlemen doing about it?' And he continued in that way for quite a few minutes. Both Venky and I took down everything he said. We had a good story! And Austin by now was taking our pictures. The train began to move and soon we were at Dadar station where the train once again stopped and thousands on the platforms were shouting 'Jawaharlal Nehru ki jai!' It was then that I heard him for the first time responding with the Indian National Army (INA) battle cry: 'Jai Hind!'

Came 14 August 1947. It was my privilege to cover what happened on the midnight of that 14th in Bombay and what a thrill it was to hear Nehru speak at the appointed hour of India's tryst with Destiny as India attained freedom from centuries of slavery. It was a midnight that I shall never forget. Listening to Jawaharlal speak that night was a rare experience as we bathed in instant glory.

The year passed. *The Free Press Journal* sent me to Delhi in 1949, and over a period of about eighteen months I listened to Jawaharlal as he addressed the Constituent Assembly; I attended his press conferences and always it was a thrill to feel I was there.

In 1955, the Press Trust of India (PTI) appointed me as its United Nations correspondent and once again an opportunity came my way to see Jawaharlal in person. He came to New York to address the UN General Assembly in September 1956. At the UN then there were just two of us Indian correspondents, I was representing the PTI and Krishna Balaraman, *The Hindu*. To cover Nehru's visit to the US, two other senior correspondents had arrived, Prem Bhatia of *The Statesman* and S. Mulgaonkar of *The Times of India*. Together, all four of us sought audience with the prime minister. It was refused. He would not see us. He would not see us in New York. He would not see us in Washington, next on the list. He would not recognize us at a press conference he held in the US capital. He would not see us in President Eisenhower's home on his estate at Gettysberg, even when the President personally took each of us around his estate in his golf cart which he himself drove! A couple of days later we were all to fly in a special plane to the Canadian capital Ottawa but still Jawaharlal would not care to talk to us. All four of us correspondents were received graciously by the Canadian Prime Minister Louis St Lawrent in his office. He wanted to know whether we had spoken to our prime minister. When we said 'No' and drew long faces, he said 'You haven't been able to see your own Prime Minister for ten days? Don't worry. I will introduce you to him. He is due here any minute' and he pushed us into a closet.

A couple of minutes passed and then Jawaharlal was announced. He had hardly walked in when the Canadian Prime Minister called out for us, saying 'Come out, boys! Meet your Prime Minister!' Nehru looked very peeved. A photo was taken of all of us. I was standing to Panditji's right.

Much the same happened to me when I covered the first Non-aligned Conference held in Belgrade in 1961. I was the only Indian reporter—the only Asian one, for that matter—to cover the meeting, attended by some twenty international leaders, including Soekarno of Indonesia, Nasser of Egypt and Marshal Tito of Yugoslavia. I could get access to them but not to Jawaharlal, my own Prime Minister! I have never understood that. And that was the last time I saw him in person.

Looking back I keep wondering why Nehru was so reluctant to meet Indian journalists who were serving abroad for Indian newspapers. We were not the ones to show familiarity, far from it. We held him in awe; at least I did. He met European and American correspondents freely which was understandable. I have been similarly received by European and American leaders. Was it because he felt socially superior to us and felt it below his dignity to meet us? When I meet him in Heaven—I am sure I will be there even if I have been a journalist! I would have only one question to ask him 'Panditji, why were you so disdainful towards us? Why were you so determined to keep us at arms' length? Weren't we just doing our job?'

As an ordinary citizen I had no political differences with Jawaharlalji. Like many of my generation, I supported him fully. In the late 1930s and 1940s, socialism was the fashion of the day. Though Jawaharlal was very much a socialist at heart, he never joined the Congress Socialist Party of which many, like Jayaprakash Narayan, Achyut Patwardhan, Yusuf Meherally, even Narendra Deva, Prakasha, N.G. Ranga, and Sampurnananda were members. That did not bother me. His demand at the Congress Party's Madras (now Chennai) session for the establishment of a 'socialistic pattern of society' was hailed by the youth of my generation. We applauded Nehru's setting up of the Indian Institutes of Technology (IITs) and Indian Institutes of Management (IIMs) as well as his zest for building dams. At that point in time—the late 1940s and early 1950s—capitalism was a no-no. It was only as we grew older—and hopefully wiser—that political sense began to dawn on us. Nehru, in his time, could not have been anything else except a socialist. If in his days he preferred socialism to liberal capitalism and was proved wrong, we who supported him should admit to our guilt as well.

Did Nehru commit mistakes? Looking back I feel he did. He should under no circumstances have taken the Kashmir issue to the UN Security Council. He should have waited for the Indian Army to capture Lahore and then ask Pakistan to come to terms. By taking the issue to the Security Council he made the biggest mistake of his life for which the nation is still paying.

Second, he should have readily accepted the offer made to India way back in 1945 of Permanent Membership of the Security Council when it was given to him on a golden platter. He had then declined the offer saying that China better deserved the offer. That was just as big a folly as his decision on the Kashmir issue.

Third, he should have known better than to accept V.K. Krishna Menon as his advisor on international affairs. It was not just a wrong choice. It was a bad choice. And he paid for it.

Fourth, he should never have conceded that Tibet was an integral part of China. He should have maintained a discreet silence on the issue, leaving the Chinese to guess. By conceding China's suzerainty over Tibet he wasted a trump card.

Nehru's disdain of Hinduism bothered me. His efforts to keep himself aloof from the rebuilding of the Somnath Temple offended me. But he was a man of his times, the last Englishman to rule India. He meant well. He was overwhelmingly a patriot. He faced imprisonment longer than, probably, any of his contemporaries. That was a fantastic sacrifice. But his Last Will and Testament, his graphic, almost poetic reference to Ganga endeared him to me. According to *A Centenary History of the Indian National Congress* (Vol. II),

Jawaharlal Nehru was highly spiritual without being religious and was determined to construct his life on the foundation of ethical values imbibed from various sources. It is against this background that his ideas on Marxism and social ideology ought to be tested. Besides, he responded to the concept of socialism through nationalism and sought to adapt socialism to suit Indian conditions and the Indian genius.

In a conversation with a European correspondent, Tibor Mende in 1956, he spelt out how Gandhiji's influence filtered down to him in day-to-day life. He recalled—and that is the best way to end this article:

The effect of Gandhiji on me in the early days was to simplify my life very much. I gave up eating meat. That had nothing to do with philosophy. It just simplified my existence and a slight touch of austerity also came in with it. The kind of influence Gandhi had on vast numbers of people. It changed the whole manner of our living. Again, I had read the *Gita* occasionally and admired it. I read it *again and again*. Not for a philosophical or from a theosophical point of view, but it had numerous parts which had a powerful effect on me. The sort of thing that if a person does the right thing, the right results will flow from it ...

Though I had witnessed Jawaharlal's activities, listened to his talks, heard him in the Parliament and at press conferences, though I have read him widely, I do not think I know him at all. He was a very complex character. To have come of age around 1935 and been a witness to the political scene in India right up to Jawaharlal's death has been a rich experience. India needed him as it needed the Mahatma. They were both unique in their own ways. If there was no Mahatma and no Jawaharlal we would have needed to invent them. That said, what else need be said?

Contributors

P.C. ALEXANDER A distinguished public servant who was Secretary to the Prime Minister, India's High Commissioner to the UK, Governor of Tamil Nadu and Maharashtra, and till recently a member of the Rajya Sabha.

MUCHKUND DUBEY An illustrious member of the Indian Foreign Service who rose to become India's Foreign Secretary. Also a well-known scholar who taught at the School of International Studies, Jawaharlal Nehru University, New Delhi.

JAGMOHAN A distinguished public servant who became the Lt. Governor of Delhi at a very young age. He served as the Governor of Jammu and Kashmir twice. He has authored several books and was awarded the Padma Shri in 1971 and the Padma Bhushan in 1977.

M.V. KAMATH One of the senior-most journalists of India who has had a long career as a reporter, foreign correspondent, and editor. He has authored over 40 books and was awarded the Padma Bhushan in 2004.

SUBHASH KASHYAP   A former Secretary General of the Lok Sabha, he is the author of the six-volume study titled *History of the Parliament of India.* He was the member of the Constitution Review Committee and Secretary General of the Lok Sabha. He has been a Jawaharlal Nehru Fellow and has received 'Vidur Samman', 'Rajiv Smriti Samman', 'Vidhi Seva Samman', and the 'Vishist Seva Award'.

INDER MALHOTRA   A senior journalist of the country who is a former editor of *The Times of India*, New Delhi, and a former *Guardian* correspondent in India. He is now a syndicated columnist and political commentator.

BALRAJ PURI   A leading Indian political commentator and human rights activist. He began his career in journalism in 1942 and has, since then, authored and edited several publications. He has played the important role of the mediator in the famous 1975 Sheikh Abdullah-Indira Gandhi accord. He is constantly consulted on various aspects of the Kashmir issue. He was conferred the Padma Bhushan in 2005.

KARAN SINGH   Former Sadr-e-Riyasat of Jammu and Kashmir, former Union Minister, and former Ambassador to the United States, he is presently a member of the Rajya Sabha and Chairman of the Indian Council for Cultural Relations. A renowned scholar of Indian philosophy, he was awarded the Padma Vibhushan in 2005.

K. NATWAR SINGH   A distinguished member of the Indian Foreign Service and a former Minister of External Affairs, he led the Indian delegation to the 42nd session of the UN General Assembly. He was awarded the Padma Bhushan in 1984.